D1600906

812.54 I95D   c.1
Ives, David.
Don Juan in Chicago

PROPERTY OF
HIGH POINT PUBLIC LIBRARY
HIGH POINT, NORTH CAROLINA

Photo by James Leynse

Simon Brooking and Jay Smith-Cameron in the Primary Stages production of "Don Juan in Chicago." Set design by Bob Phillips.

DON JUAN
IN CHICAGO

BY DAVID IVES

★

★

DRAMATISTS
PLAY SERVICE
INC.

PROPERTY OF
HIGH POINT PUBLIC LIBRARY
HIGH POINT, NORTH CAROLINA

DON JUAN IN CHICAGO
Copyright © 1995, David Ives

All Rights Reserved

CAUTION: Professionals and amateurs are hereby warned that performance of DON JUAN IN CHICAGO is subject to a royalty. It is fully protected under the copyright laws of the United States of America, and of all countries covered by the International Copyright Union (including the Dominion of Canada and the rest of the British Commonwealth), and of all countries covered by the Pan-American Copyright Convention, the Universal Copyright Convention, the Berne Convention, and of all countries with which the United States has reciprocal copyright relations. All rights, including professional/amateur stage rights, motion picture, recitation, lecturing, public reading, radio broadcasting, television, video or sound recording, all other forms of mechanical or electronic reproduction, such as CD-ROM, CD-I, information storage and retrieval systems and photocopying, and the rights of translation into foreign languages, are strictly reserved. Particular emphasis is placed upon the matter of readings, permission for which must be secured from the Author's agent in writing.

The stage performance rights in DON JUAN IN CHICAGO (other than first class rights) are controlled exclusively by the DRAMATISTS PLAY SERVICE, INC., 440 Park Avenue South, New York, N.Y. 10016. No professional or non-professional performance of the Play (excluding first class professional performance) may be given without obtaining in advance the written permission of the DRAMATISTS PLAY SERVICE, INC., and paying the requisite fee.

Inquiries concerning all other rights should be addressed to William Craver, c/o Writers & Artists Agency, 19 West 44th Street, suite 1000, New York, N.Y. 10036.

SPECIAL NOTE

Anyone receiving permission to produce DON JUAN IN CHICAGO is required to give credit to the Author as sole and exclusive Author of the Play on the title page of all programs distributed in connection with performances of the Play and in all instances in which the title of the Play appears for purposes of advertising, publicizing or otherwise exploiting the Play and/or a production thereof. The name of the Author must appear on a separate line, in which no other name appears, immediately beneath the title and in size of type equal to 50% of the largest, most prominent letter used for the title of the Play. No person, firm or entity may receive credit larger or more prominent than that accorded the Author.

2

this play is for
Casey Childs

DON JUAN IN CHICAGO received its premiere at Primary Stages (Casey Childs, Artistic Director), in New York City, in March, 1995. It was directed by Robert Stanton; the set design was by Bob Phillips; the costume design was by Jennifer von Mayrhauser; the lighting design was by Deborah Constantine; the music and sound design were by David van Tieghem; the props were by Deirdre Brennan; the fight direction was by B.H. Barry and the production stage manager was Christine Catti. The cast was as follows:

DON JUAN .... Simon Brooking
LEPORELLO .... Larry Block
MEPHISTOPHELES .... Peter Bartlett
DONA ELVIRA .... J. Smith-Cameron
SANDY .... Nancy Opel
TODD .... T. Scott Cunningham
MIKE .... Mark Setlock
ZOEY .... Dina Spybey

DON JUAN IN CHICAGO

ACT ONE

Seville

Spain, 1599. Lightning and thunder, as lights come up on a chamber in Don Juan's palace: a door to the outside, a window up right.

Don Juan — 30, handsome, wearing a severe black doublet and ruff — is mixing a blood-red liquid from a recipe in an enormous ancient book. On the worktable before him, alchemical flasks are bubbling. A skull is also on the table. A pentagram is drawn on the floor. One wall of this chamber is shelves of books.

DON JUAN. *Sanguis melanchrys bovis atque caput avis ... (Lightning and thunder.) Lingua serpentis et folium floris. Commiscite! (Louder lightning and thunder. Knocking at door.)*
LEPORELLO. *(Offstage.)* Don Juan! Hello! Don Juan? *(Don Juan pays no attention.)*
DON JUAN. *Crepusculi pulvis et lacrima virginis ...(More knocking.)*
LEPORELLO. *(Offstage.)* Master? Master, I know you're in there!
DON JUAN. *Canis capillus et capillus regis. Admiscete!*
LEPORELLO. *(Offstage.)* Hey, BOSS! Open up! *(More knocking, more lightning and thunder.)*
DON JUAN. *Ranae membrana et oculus felis. Incipite! (Leporello enters, with a food tray.)*
LEPORELLO. Don Juan.

DON JUAN. Leporello?

LEPORELLO. Whatever you're doing, take a break.

DON JUAN. *Arcesso te! Advoco te! Impero te! Adesto! (The loudest thunder yet. Then the storm abates.)*

LEPORELLO. Maybe you didn't notice, señor. It's the end of the world out there today.

DON JUAN. It's not the end, Leporello. It's the beginning!

LEPORELLO. Oh, forsooth? Well for the moment what we got is a large red cloud raining down ashes, burning sulfur, and snakes.

DON JUAN. Excellent.

LEPORELLO. And the ashes and the sulfur and the snakes — Hello, master! — they're only falling on *this palace,* Don Juan.

DON JUAN. I'll bet they are.

LEPORELLO. The next street over? It's brilliant sunshine! The rest of Seville? The roses are in bloom! Here? I got reptiles blowing in my windows.

DON JUAN. *(Consults book.)* "Set hourglass to five minutes and let simmer." *(Don Juan turns over a large hourglass.)* You only have until these sands run out.

LEPORELLO. Question, sire.

DON JUAN. And then you're going to have to leave.

LEPORELLO. This alchemistry set you got here — this couldn't have anything to do with the reptilian drizzle we're having today...?

DON JUAN. Leporello, what I'm doing here is the greatest experiment in the history of mankind.

LEPORELLO. Oh, I see.

DON JUAN. On wings of magic I'll mount above the reach of any man that's gone before!

LEPORELLO. *(To the audience.)* The village idiot. *(Noticing.)* MOTHER OF JESUS! Is that a *PENTAGRAM?!*

DON JUAN. It's part of the experiment.

LEPORELLO. *(Rubbing it out with his foot.)* You want the Grand Inquisitor knocking on our door?

DON JUAN. *(Pulling him away.)* Don't do that, Leporello.

LEPORELLO. What the hell are you doing here, anyway?

DON JUAN.   I'm calling up Satan.

LEPORELLO.   Oh. The Prince of Darkness is dropping by today?

DON JUAN.   It's perfectly safe.

LEPORELLO.   Sure, sure. Remember the flying machine? *(Dive-bombing crash motion with his hand.)* Aero Don Juan?

DON JUAN.   The wings made it too heavy.

LEPORELLO.   Plus me inside it — ?

DON JUAN.   A miscalculation.

LEPORELLO.   Or the artificial cow?

DON JUAN.   I got some milk out of it.

LEPORELLO.   And poisoned the cat.

DON JUAN.   But this is the greatest experiment in the history of —

LEPORELLO.   *(Cutting in.)* Yeah, yeah, yeah. *Mankind.* Listen, three days now you haven't eaten. Why don't you take a break and have some lunch. *(Munches a piece of toast.)* Mmmm! Delicious!

DON JUAN.   I really don't understand what's so important about food.

LEPORELLO.   Master.

DON JUAN.   Leporello?

LEPORELLO.   Can we talk man to almost-man here?

DON JUAN.   I can't be responsible if you're here when Satan arrives.

LEPORELLO.   *(To audience.)* They should put him in a home. *(To Don Juan.)* My prince, how old are you these days?

DON JUAN.   29. No — 30 now.

LEPORELLO.   Happy birthday. So you're 30, you're rich, you're handsome, you have your health. You also still have your virginity. Or am I mistaken?

DON JUAN.   As far as I know.

LEPORELLO.   *Mi amigo,* the world is your cloister. Why don't you pay your debt to biology and get yourself a girlfriend. Discover the joys of genital stimulation. Otherwise you're gonna get a prostate the size of a tomato.

DON JUAN.   Life is too short to waste it on sex.

LEPORELLO.   No, life is short so gather ye gonads while ye

may.

DON JUAN.   I just don't see the point of carnal relations.

LEPORELLO.   Look around you, señor! *(Don Juan starts to look around.)* No, I mean get outa this room and *then* look around and what are you gonna see? *People — shtupping — everywhere.*

DON JUAN.   Not in public — ?

LEPORELLO.   No not in public but showing up in public with silly grins on their faces, which is the same thing. Women with this *glow.* Have you ever seen that glow?

DON JUAN.   I have seen that glow.

LEPORELLO.   Sex, pal.

DON JUAN.   Really.

LEPORELLO.   Everywhere and all the time, naked and clothed, night and day, man and beast are engaged in this strange and wonderful activity. And why?

DON JUAN.   I guess it's a mystery.

LEPORELLO.   Because it's WONNNNNNNDERFUL.

DON JUAN.   And women actually allow themselves to undergo this bestial activity?

LEPORELLO.   Somehow they do. How do you think you got here? Your mother glowed. Your father grinned. Why can't you?

DON JUAN.   Life was slower back then.

LEPORELLO.   I pick the snakes out of your chimney twenty-nine hours a day, and yet I find time to dip my strawberry.

DON JUAN.   I don't know where.

LEPORELLO.   In the scullery, with Allison the milkmaid.

DON JUAN.   No I mean where do you find the time.

LEPORELLO.   Oh God, Allison, sweet Allison the milkmaid, created on the same day as butter and cream! And you sit here while such creatures are loose? Wake up and smell the pollen! Did you notice the babe in the third row, by the way?

DON JUAN.   Yes. Very pretty.

LEPORELLO.   *(Waving into audience.)* Hiya, honey. — Look, Don, look!

DON JUAN.   *(To Woman in audience.)* I apologize for my servant, señora.

LEPORELLO.   Don't worry, they love it. Doesn't she make your hormones moan just a little louder?

DON JUAN.   Yes, of course, women are attractive. But to go through all the work of locating a suitable woman and then spending weeks and months pursuing her?

LEPORELLO.   What work? You're Don Juan de Tenorio y Saavedra! You don't have to pursue! They'll locate *you!* Dona Elvira walks by here twenty times a day. *(That's pronounced "El-veer-a.")* Looking up at the windows. Batting the lashes. Fanning, fanning. Where do you think that breeze always comes from? Moving those hips that say, *"yes, yes, yes."*

DON JUAN.   But so many woman only seem to be interested in the most superficial things. Clothing, and jewelry ...

LEPORELLO.   Hey, hey, hey. This is the 16th century, what do you want? Women don't have any *outlets.*

DON JUAN.   They don't?

LEPORELLO.   No. They're repressed by bastards like us!

DON JUAN.   So it's a social issue.

LEPORELLO.   And this is where you come in. Help womankind to a better future, my magnanimous master. Locate a person of the female persuasion. Talk about Plato with her, instead of with me, who doesn't give a shit. Give her a chance to realize her potential as a unique human individual. And then sleep with her at every possible opportunity. It's a great deal! Totally symbiotic!

DON JUAN.   But surely we were given this emerald earth to better purpose than placing loin to hairy loin.

LEPORELLO.   Well when you put it like that ...

DON JUAN.   If I could find a woman who knew poetry ...

LEPORELLO.   You'd sleep with her — ?

DON JUAN.   I could discuss art with her.

LEPORELLO.   And sleep with her.

DON JUAN.   Talk about the life of the spirit.

LEPORELLO.   And sleep with her.

DON JUAN.   Leporello.

LEPORELLO.   Sleep with her.

DON JUAN.   Do you know what this is? *(He holds up the skull.)*

LEPORELLO. The sickest paperweight in Seville.

DON JUAN. This was once a man like you.

LEPORELLO. Better paid, I bet.

DON JUAN. All the things you see around us are passing out of the world. They're dying. They're unimportant.

LEPORELLO. So what are we supposed to do, bury ourselves alive? Climb in and pull the dirt over, save the funeral expenses?

DON JUAN. Do you know what's truly important in this world?

LEPORELLO. Fellatio?

DON JUAN. Knowledge.

LEPORELLO. Eesh.

DON JUAN. The life of the mind.

LEPORELLO. Ogh!

DON JUAN. Eternal truth.

LEPORELLO. You're a *freak*.

DON JUAN. A spirit is trapped inside this walking cage of bone, and it wants to know what it's doing here.

LEPORELLO. *(Holds out a crust.)* Eat.

DON JUAN. No thank you.

LEPORELLO. You're not a man, you're a windmill. And the blades are turning, but they're not hooked up inside. Get normal, will ya, Don Juan? And please, *please* — give me a raise.

DON JUAN. You just got a raise.

LEPORELLO. Seven years ago. *(A flash of lightning outside.)*

DON JUAN. The sands have run out. You have to go now. *(Busies himself with the flasks again.)*

LEPORELLO. Tyrant.

DON JUAN. I can't be responsible if you stay.

LEPORELLO. Oh, sure. I start talking wages and suddenly you're not responsible. Because the *boogie man* is dropping by. *(We have started to hear an ominous rumbling.)*

DON JUAN. Leporello, you have to leave!

LEPORELLO. I demand a cost-of-living increase! *(The rumbling is getting louder. A mystical chorus of voices. More lightning and thunder.)*

DON JUAN. Leave, Leporello! *Go!*

LEPORELLO.   And turn off the snakes! *(Leporello exits. Don Juan stands in the center of the pentagram.)*
DON JUAN.   *In nomine omnium nefariorum imperiorum impero te! Coniuro te! Appareat et surgat — Mephistophilis! (The storm climaxes in a deafening thunderclap, and in a puff of smoke, Mephistopheles appears. A cosmopolitan fellow. The lightning, the thunder and the mystical chorus suddenly stop, and all is still. Mephistopheles coughs from the smoke.)*

Are you — are you — Lord Mephistopheles...?
MEPHISTOPHELES.

At your worship's service, if you please.
(He steps toward the Don.)
DON JUAN.

Keep off, Satan! *Avaunt!*

Thou canst not touch me in this pentagram!
MEPHISTOPHELES.

I'm sorry. Is this Seville, or Amsterdam?
DON JUAN.   *(Spanish: "Seh-vee-ah.")*

Sevilla.
MEPHISTOPHELES.

You did call me, I believe.
DON JUAN.

That was the idea.
MEPHISTOPHELES.

Thank — I won't say God — I'm relieved.

I hate arriving at the wrong door.
(He coughs.)
DON JUAN.

I've never called up a fantasma before!
(Mephistopheles coughs.)

Are you all right?
MEPHISTOPHELES.

Asthma. *(Cough.)* What a bore.

The smoke can make these entrances rough.

What's the local time, just off the cuff?
DON JUAN.

May, 1599. No — June.

11

MEPHISTOPHELES.
>Ah-ha. Morning?

DON JUAN.
>Afternoon.
>
>I think. I've never been very good about time.
>
>But can I offer you some food? A glass of wine?

MEPHISTOPHELES.
>Thank you, but alas. Spirit, you know.
>
>Pleasures of the flesh
>
>Are inaccessible to beings who go to and fro
>
>In the superphysical milieu.

DON JUAN.
>And yet you have asthma?

MEPHISTOPHELES.
>*I* can't explain it. Can you?

DON JUAN.
>Well you did revolt against the king of heaven.

MEPHISTOPHELES.
>It's true.

DON JUAN.
>In all his might and glory.

MEPHISTOPHELES.
>A complicated story. *Eeeuw.*

(Mephistopheles has noticed the skull.)

DON JUAN.
>Oh that. A paperweight of mine.
>
>Maybe sort of foolish.

MEPHISTOPHELES.
>Not to mention sort of ...

DON JUAN.
>Ghoulish?
>
>I find it rather stirring, myself,
>
>To contemplate the bone.

MEPHISTOPHELES.
>Well, to each his own.
>
>But step out of that ridiculous geometry, milord.
>
>Be brave!

DON JUAN.
>You won't harm me?

MEPHISTOPHELES.   *(Crossing his heart.)*
>I swear it on my mother's grave.

(Don Juan steps out of the pentagram.)
>But to tell you true, Don Juan,
>I was shocked, *shocked,* to hear from such a paragon
>As you.
>Why on earth could you want old devious me?

DON JUAN.
>Are we acquainted ... previously?

MEPHISTOPHELES.
>Oh I like to keep up on possible clients.
>Princes, clergy, literary lions ...
>Folks who'd pawn their immortal soul
>For some quick delight.

(Looking into the audience.)
>I see some prospects are with us tonight.*
>But not to be overly imperial,
>You never seemed like my kind of material.
>A man with everything from gold to great ability.
>A man who even has his original virginity,
>Or am I mistaken?

DON JUAN.
>No, that's still intact.

MEPHISTOPHELES.
>Hard on the prostate, it's a fact.
>But I presume I'm here to dicker for your soul?

DON JUAN.
>If you're willing to take on the role.

MEPHISTOPHELES.
>*Enchanté.*

DON JUAN.
>And if I can.

* On matinee days: "... For some instant boon/I see some prospects are with us this afternoon."

MEPHISTOPHELES.

    I'm honored to be dealing with an intelligent man.
    Because I tell you, Don Juan, tinkers and tailors,
    Cabbies and kings —
    People will sell their souls for the stupidest things
    These days. Trinkets and trifles —
    You name it, they'll ask it.
    This world is going to hell *for* a handbasket.
    Last week, I got a summons from a baker in
        Hamburg.
    He conjures me up. The ashes, the sulfur —

DON JUAN.

    — the snakes —

MEPHISTOPHELES.

    — *and* the wheeze —
    This Teutonic barbarian cries, "Take my soul, please!
    Move earth and heaven! Use all your magic!"
    And what does he want? A *new oven*.

DON JUAN.

    It's tragic.

MEPHISTOPHELES.

    And idiots like that come a dime a dozen!
    The man's a clown!

DON JUAN.

    But you took him up?

MEPHISTOPHELES.

    I turned him *down*, of course.
    Where's the challenge? Where's the art?
    I said to this oaf, "Take hearth.
    Bake a better loaf
    And you can *buy* a second bakery."
    Take his soul in exchange for a stove?
    It cheapens my work to a kind of ...

DON JUAN.

    Fakery.

MEPHISTOPHELES.

    Bravo. If you want to go to hell for all eternity,

Have a little gumption.
Go the usual way, through sin and corruption.
Human stupidity truly startles me.
O what tools these mortals be.
But I got off the track.
Please excuse me.
You Who Have Everything — pray,
How can you use me?

DON JUAN.
　　It's true, as you say, that I have lots.
MEPHISTOPHELES.
　　You have unlimited money.
DON JUAN.
　　I have pots!
　　Yet I still lack one crucial ...
MEPHISTOPHELES.
　　Element?
DON JUAN.
　　Dimension.
MEPHISTOPHELES.
　　The tension
　　Is killing, but let me guess, let me guess.
　　Is it something invisible?
DON JUAN.
　　Yes.
　　You might call it everyone's greatest hope.
MEPHISTOPHELES.
　　You want to be pope.
DON JUAN.
　　Nope.
MEPHISTOPHELES.
　　Sorry. A personal kink.
　　But wait a second, let me think ...
　　Magic powers? Some all-powerful mantra?
DON JUAN.
　　No.
MEPHISTOPHELES.
　　You want to sleep with Cleopantra.

DON JUAN.

> No.

MEPHISTOPHELES.

> The Midas touch, turn lead into gold?

DON JUAN.

> You're cold, you're cold.

MEPHISTOPHELES.

> You want to commit the perfect crime.
>
> Murder an heiress?

DON JUAN.

> No what I want.... But now I'm embarrassed.

MEPHISTOPHELES.

> Just tell me.

DON JUAN.

> I know you're going to chortle.

MEPHISTOPHELES.

> I promise I won't.

DON JUAN.

> Well. I want to be immortal.

MEPHISTOPHELES.

> Immortal. That's interesting ...

DON JUAN.

> I know it's a bit much.

MEPHISTOPHELES.

> No, no, not as such.
>
> But I have my limits, despite what you hear.
>
> I can't turn you into Dante
>
> Or — who's that fairy? — Shakespeare.
>
> But please, persev'er.

DON JUAN.

> I mean immortal as in time.
>
> I want to live forever.

MEPHISTOPHELES.

> Ah-ha. *That* kind.

DON JUAN.

> Here I am 29 — no, 30 years old,
>
> Middle age is brewing,
>
> And I haven't done a single thing worth doing.

Three decades and nothing to show for it —
Why *shouldn't* I sell my soul?

MEPHISTOPHELES.

Go for it.

DON JUAN.

When I think what I could do if I never died!
Why, I could discover the meaning of life!
The eternal truths of time,
What the basis of the cosmos is!
If not by study, then —

MEPHISTOPHELES.

By osmosis.

DON JUAN.

I could measure every peak, plumb every ocean,
Try every crazy thought and extravagant notion.
I might create a universal tongue.

MEPHISTOPHELES.

You *might* explain what's wrong with my lungs.

DON JUAN.

I could read all the great books.

MEPHISTOPHELES.

Twice.

DON JUAN.

I might even have time for women.

MEPHISTOPHELES.

Might be nice.

DON JUAN.

See if love is all it's cracked up to be.

MEPHISTOPHELES.

It's always been a mystery to *me.*

DON JUAN.

I could try my hand at verse, or sculpt in clay —

MEPHISTOPHELES.

You might do worse, and write a play.

DON JUAN.

I could become a household name!
"Don Juan" could be a synonym for brain!

MEPHISTOPHELES.
>   Unless another organ brings you fame.
DON JUAN.
>   Excuse me?
MEPHISTOPHELES.
>   I can't guarantee which part of your anatomy
>   Gilds your immortality.
DON JUAN.
>   I wasn't meant for this benighted age,
>   Rotten from titled lord to dog-eared page.
>   I want to live to see that glorious day
>   Say four centuries hence
>   When the world won't be ruled by pesos and pence.
>   The year two thousand!
>   When humankind will wear peace's golden crest!
>   Yes. To live forever. That's my humble request.
MEPHISTOPHELES.
>   Interesting. Interesting.
>   Well, Don Juan, I don't want to trick you, but ...
DON JUAN.
>   Do you think...?
MEPHISTOPHELES.
>   Oh, I think I can fix you. I mean, fix you up.
DON JUAN.
>   Fantastic!
MEPHISTOPHELES.
>   Though it wouldn't be free.
>   There is a quid pro quo.
DON JUAN.
>   To sell you my soul?
MEPHISTOPHELES.
>   The traditional fee.
DON JUAN.
>   But that's where my plan is so wonderful!
>   You want me to gamble my soul
>   And I'll willingly bet it
>   Because if I live forever, you'll never get it!

MEPHISTOPHELES.

Technically. You see your soul is not the quid pro quo.

Your soul is just the ... escrow.

(He magically produces a piece of paper.)

DON JUAN.

A contract, already?

MEPHISTOPHELES.

These things are boilerplate. Standard as hymns.

DON JUAN.

"DAMNATION AGREEMENT."

MEPHISTOPHELES.

Oh I know it sounds grim.

Just look it over and sign where it says ...

DON JUAN.

"Victim"?

MEPHISTOPHELES.

A printing error.

Cross that out, we'll correct it later.

(There is a knock at the door.)

LEPORELLO.   *(Offstage.)*

Hey, Don Juan!

DON JUAN.

Leporello? *(Leporello enters.)*

LEPORELLO.

Did El Diablo ever find you?

DON JUAN.

Yes, he's standing right behind you.

LEPORELLO.

Oooh, I'm shaking. I'm *Jell-O.*

But maybe His Darkness would like a liqueur,

Or a bubbly with lime?

DON JUAN.

Leporello, could you come back another time?

LEPORELLO.

Oh sure!

The hell am I doing talking in rhyme...?

DON JUAN.

Maybe later, since we're secluded?

19

I want to get the work in hand ...

LEPORELLO.

Concluded. I understand.

(To audience.)

This guy is deluded! He's a goddamn psychopath!

(Starts out.)

Adios, Mephisto! Blow it out your ath!

DON JUAN.

Uh, Leporello ...

LEPORELLO.

See you in hell, ya dink!

(Leporello exits.)

MEPHISTOPHELES.

It might happen sooner than he thinks.

DON JUAN.

Sorry about that. He's not malign.

MEPHISTOPHELES.

No problem. Happens all the time.

DON JUAN.

But you said you might get my soul.

Can you give me a hint?

MEPHISTOPHELES.

Well it's hard to explain —

DON JUAN.

What's this small print?

Oh no. You have to be kidding.

MEPHISTOPHELES.

Just a condition to spice up the bidding.

DON JUAN.

"Don Juan agrees

To seduce a different woman *every day*" — ?!

MEPHISTOPHELES.

And if you don't sleep with a woman by midnight,

I come and take you away.

DON JUAN.

To hell?

MEPHISTOPHELES.

That's right.

DON JUAN.

    For eternal torment.

MEPHISTOPHELES.

    Oh pshaw, man! Hell's a mere formality!

    A straw man!

DON JUAN.

    Hmm ...

MEPHISTOPHELES.

    Regular sex is a pittance to pay for immortality.

    Pricks one's interest, wouldn't you say?

DON JUAN.

    But a different woman every day?

MEPHISTOPHELES.

    And no woman twice. That's the sum of it.

DON JUAN.

    Sort of challenging.

MEPHISTOPHELES.

    That's the fun of it!

    And once you get the knack, it's easy as pie.

DON JUAN.

    But I've never seduced a woman!

MEPHISTOPHELES.

    Just get down on your knees and lie.

DON JUAN.

    Yes, but ...

MEPHISTOPHELES.

    You're after the biggest of game, Don Juan!

    Who cares if you have to *chercher la femme?*

DON JUAN.

    I could always pay a woman to agree.

MEPHISTOPHELES.

    Um, sorry — Clause 23.

    The sex must be free and without compunction.

DON JUAN.

    But I don't know anything about seduction!

    I haven't grown up on it!

MEPHISTOPHELES.

    Then you'll have all eternity to bone up on it.

So to speak. As long as every day
You arouse and sate a woman's lust.
DON JUAN.

Yes, but if I don't ...
MEPHISTOPHELES.

Poof!
DON JUAN.

Dust.
MEPHISTOPHELES. *(Taking the contract away.)*

But if you don't want to sign, I can't force you to it.
DON JUAN.

No, fine.
(Takes it back.)
MEPHISTOPHELES.

I'd really understand.
DON JUAN.

No, no. Let's do it.
MEPHISTOPHELES.

A more generous offer could not be made.
DON JUAN.

Do I have to sign in blood?
MEPHISTOPHELES.

A given, I'm afraid.

An enigma — like my asthma.

So hold out a finger and let's draw some plasma.
DON JUAN.   *(Holds out his middle finger.)*

This one?
MEPHISTOPHELES.

Most apropos. Let's give it a blood test.
(Mephistopheles slices a blade across it, drawing blood, and a sudden gasp from Don Juan.)

Bravo.
(Mephistopheles takes a quill pen, dips the point into the tip of the finger, and holds out the pen.)

Be my guest.
(The Don is about to sign, but stops.)
DON JUAN.

But what about Leporello?

MEPHISTOPHELES.
>   You mean the fellow...?
DON JUAN.
>   Outside, my hired man.
>   I'll need someone to keep things spic-and-span
>   While I'm — you know —
>   Discovering eternal truths and seducing women.
MEPHISTOPHELES.
>   We could always write him in —
>   If you don't mind making him immortal too.
DON JUAN.
>   Without his consent?
MEPHISTOPHELES.
>   He's only a servant.
DON JUAN.
>   It's true.
>   Where do I sign?
MEPHISTOPHELES.
>   Anywhere's fine.
(To audience.)
>   The man is a fool.
(Don Juan dips the pen-point into the tip of his finger, and Mephistopheles turns so the Don can put the contract on his back while he signs.)
>   And somehow I doubt this *paraquito*
>   Will be getting lots of rest.
>   How are you doing, m'lord?
DON JUAN.
>   *Finito! Consummatum est!*
MEPHISTOPHELES.
>   Lovely. Congratulations.
(He rolls up the contract.)
DON JUAN.
>   So. When does it begin?
MEPHISTOPHELES.
>   Begin?
DON JUAN.
>   I mean, eternity.

MEPHISTOPHELES.

Oh it's begun.

DON JUAN.

You mean — already?

MEPHISTOPHELES.

It's done. My metaphysical gambler.

DON JUAN.

I'm immortal?

MEPHISTOPHELES.

Fixed like a fly in amber.

DON JUAN.

But I don't feel any change.

MEPHISTOPHELES.

You never will. You'll never age.

You have stopped, while all the universe

Around you moves faster and faster.

DON JUAN.

I don't know how to thank you.

MEPHISTOPHELES.

Oh no need to thank me.

Just call me ... master.

(Suddenly there's a thunderclap, and that chorus of mystical voices.)
Redeo, ferae nefandae! Aperite, O portae! Recipe, O Tantare, tuum
regem! Accipe me Mephistophelem!
(And with a cough — he's gone. In a moment, the storm is over and
the darkness outside the window turns to spring sunshine.)

DON JUAN.   So. I'm immortal now. I'm immortal! I'm going to live forever! *(Tiny pause.)* What now? *(Calls.) Leporello?*
LEPORELLO! *(Leporello enters.)*

LEPORELLO.   My liege?

DON JUAN.   What time is it?

LEPORELLO.   I don't know, five o'clock. So how was your
visit with "Satan"?

DON JUAN.   Wonderful.

LEPORELLO.   Something burning in here...?

DON JUAN.   My servant.

LEPORELLO.   Yes, bwana?

DON JUAN.   I have to find a woman.

24

LEPORELLO.   Excellent! Congratulations! *(Pumps the Don's hand.)* Is that a hard-on? I beg your pard-on.

DON JUAN.   Very funny. The thing is, I have to find this woman by midnight tonight.

LEPORELLO.   It's about time.

DON JUAN.   And another woman by midnight tomorrow.

LEPORELLO.   Really going for it, huh. Well you gotta be dying of terminal horniness by now.

DON JUAN.   But that's just it! I'm not dying of *anything.* And neither are you! HA HA HA HA! We ... are not dying ... of *ANYTHING!*

LEPORELLO.   You seem slightly demented, my prince.

DON JUAN.   Well why not? *WE'RE NOT DYING ANYMORE!*

LEPORELLO.   Uh-huh. Listen. Getting back to these women ...

DON JUAN.   Yes. One woman by midnight.

LEPORELLO.   We'll go out and find you a real honey.

DON JUAN.   She doesn't have to be a honey.

LEPORELLO.   Excuse me?

DON JUAN.   She doesn't have to be beautiful. And I can give the encounter about three minutes, as soon as possible.

LEPORELLO.   *Padrone.*

DON JUAN.   Speak.

LEPORELLO.   This is your first time out?

DON JUAN.   To my knowledge.

LEPORELLO.   Wouldn't you like it to be sort of a beautiful experience?

DON JUAN.   It's not essential.

LEPORELLO.   So you'd settle for a toothless one-eyed hunchback.

DON JUAN.   Yes. Fine.

LEPORELLO.   Okay, let's see what we can scrape up. *(Doorbell, offstage.)*

DON JUAN.   Whoever it is, turn them away. I can't see anyone until I've had a woman.

LEPORELLO.   *(Looking out the window.)* But this is perfect! It's heaven-sent!

DON JUAN.   What.

LEPORELLO.   It's Dona Elvira, all oiled and perfumed. The

mountain has come to jump on Mohammed!

DON JUAN. Let her in.

LEPORELLO. But listen, you gotta spruce yourself up. *(Dusts off Don Juan's doublet.)*

DON JUAN. But Leporello?

LEPORELLO. Yes, my amorous one?

DON JUAN. What do I do?

LEPORELLO. You talk love to her!

DON JUAN. But what do I say, exactly?

LEPORELLO. Oh, the usual eternal sentiments. How beautiful she is, the minute you saw her you got carried away, you lay awake at night and burn for her ...

DON JUAN. Wait a minute. I'd better write this down. *(Scribbles on the palm of his hand.)* "Beautiful. Carried away. Lie awake at night ..."

LEPORELLO. Burn.

DON JUAN. "Burn for her ..."

LEPORELLO. She's a goddess.

DON JUAN. "Goddess ..."

LEPORELLO. You're an idiot.

DON JUAN. "Idiot ..."

LEPORELLO. Scratch that out. *(Noticing where Satan sliced him.)* Did you cut your finger?

DON JUAN. Ah, yes, I want to talk to you about that, actually ...

LEPORELLO. Also, women love getting called stuff like dove, pigeon.

DON JUAN. "Dove. Pigeon ..."

LEPORELLO. Think pet shop.

DON JUAN. "Pet shop ..." *(Doorbell.)*

LEPORELLO. I better go let her in.

DON JUAN. By the way, Leporello.

LEPORELLO. She ain't gonna wait forever.

DON JUAN. You're immortal now.

LEPORELLO. Oh. Great. *(Comes back.)* Excuse me?

DON JUAN. You're going to live forever. So am I.

LEPORELLO. Forsooth? *(To audience.)* I'm torn between letting the lady in and inquiring further.

26

DON JUAN.   I made a deal with Satan this afternoon.

LEPORELLO.   *(To Don Juan.)* Mm-hm....

DON JUAN.   Which gave us eternal life.

LEPORELLO.   Ah-ha. Does this mean I get a raise?

DON JUAN.   We can talk about that later. You'd better let Dona Elvira in.

LEPORELLO.   Wait, wait, wait. You made a deal with Satan.

DON JUAN.   That's where we drew the blood. *(Don holds up his middle finger.)*

LEPORELLO.   Can you prove this wasn't induced by the fumes in here?

DON JUAN.   *(Takes a dagger and stabs Leporello in the chest.)* Quod erat demonstrandum.

LEPORELLO.   Interesting.

DON JUAN.   Nothing can kill us as long as I stay lucky. *(He keeps stabbing Leporello in the chest.)*

LEPORELLO.   Question B. — You can stop now. — What does "luck" have to do with this, if we're immortal? And I sense we're into the nitty-gritty here, so help me out.

DON JUAN.   Well, as part of the agreement, I have to sleep with a different woman every day.

LEPORELLO.   Or — ?

DON JUAN.   Well ...

LEPORELLO.   Eternal torment? The fiery pit?

DON JUAN.   More or less.

LEPORELLO.   Sulfur and brimstone? The terminal tan?

DON JUAN.   You might say that.

LEPORELLO.   And I was somehow involved in this transaction?

DON JUAN.   You're in the contract as "personal secretary."

LEPORELLO.   Oh *good*. Oh *good*.

DON JUAN.   You always wanted a job title.

LEPORELLO.   So the skinny is, you wrote me into a contract with Satan under which you, who have never seduced even a sheep in your whole miserable life, now have to persuade a woman a *day*? YOU FUCKING MORON! YOU CRETIN!

DON JUAN.   Watch yourself.

LEPORELLO.   Oh yeah, what're you gonna do? *Kill* me?

DON JUAN. I can't. You're immortal.

LEPORELLO. Thank you. And somehow in the middle of this you never thought, "Wait a minute. Leporello might have a little input here ..."

DON JUAN. You *are* only a servant.

LEPORELLO. Oh well then! Why wait? Just toss me on the barbie right now! And there I was flipping Satan the bird. *(Babbling.)* Help me, God, help me, help me, help me!

DON JUAN. I don't think he can.

LEPORELLO. May I see this contract, please? My mad master?

DON JUAN. Well — I don't have it.

LEPORELLO. So your good buddy Lucifer has the only copy.

DON JUAN. But Dona Elvira is waiting.

LEPORELLO. And our future unto ages and ages, depends on whether this girl happens to be in the mood. It's come, or kingdom-come.

DON JUAN. At least through tomorrow.

LEPORELLO. Just tell her, "Oh by the way. If you don't sleep with me, I go to hell for all eternity." See if you score.

DON JUAN. Do you think she'd believe me?

LEPORELLO. Y'see, milord, it all depends on the foreplay.

DON JUAN. "Foreplay"...?

LEPORELLO. I'll go let her in. *(Leporello exits.)*

DON JUAN. Foreplay. Foreplay ... *(Looks in mirror, fixes his hair.)* You are immortal. But wait. *(Checks the palm of his hand.)* "Beautiful. Lie ... amurk?... awake at night. Burn. Godless idiot." Burn, godless idiot? *(Leporello enters.)*

LEPORELLO. Dona Elvira! And God bless us, every one! *(He exits as Dona Elvira sweeps in: gorgeous outfit and a fan.)*

DON JUAN. Dona Elvira.

ELVIRA.

> Don Juan! I can't believe you're safe!
> You and your vassal.

DON JUAN.

> Why shouldn't I be safe?

ELVIRA.

> Well, snakes were falling on your castle.

DON JUAN.

Ah, that. I'm sorry if they misgave you.

ELVIRA.

I thought I might drop by and save you.
Excuse me for barging in like this,
Unannounced and ... unchaperoned.

DON JUAN.

No, please.

ELVIRA.

Having sent my *duenna* on a trip to Ravenna
To buy some cologne.

DON JUAN.

It's fine.

ELVIRA.

What I mean is, we're quite, quite *alone.*

DON JUAN.

I fully understand.

ELVIRA.

You know you *might* kiss my hand.
(She holds out her hand. He kisses it. As he does so, she lowers her hand to force him to his knees.)
Oh no, but please don't kneel.

DON JUAN. *(Starting to rise.)*

Very well.

ELVIRA. *(Forcing him back down.)*

But if you must, I know how you feel.

DON JUAN.

Excuse me?

ELVIRA.

There are those moments when one is overwhelmed.
When the ship of one's life has love at the helm.
When passion obscures the way we should steer,
Ruled in equal parts by desire and — what?

DON JUAN.

Fear?

ELVIRA.

I see you understand.

DON JUAN.

    I don't think I do ...

ELVIRA.

    It's all so clear. Don't you feel it too?

DON JUAN.

    Feel what?

(He starts to rise, but she forces him back down.)

ELVIRA.

    Not yet. Be still.

    Just let me look at you, let me drink my fill

    And then be gone. Forever, my Giovanni.

DON JUAN.

    But —

ELVIRA.

    My Svengali.

DON JUAN.

    I was hoping you'd stay.

ELVIRA.

    No, truly, I must go away.

    In my heart of hearts I've already sinned

    Coming here like this, throwing caution to the wind,

    Letting passion prevail.

    I should lock myself in a convent

    And take on the simple wimple and veil.

    Someplace where I can contemplate my life,

    My unlawful lust ... and my fall.

DON JUAN.

    I don't think I ...

ELVIRA.

    Don Juan, I have been in your thrall

    Since the first day I saw you.

    My heart, my soul, my Apollo —

    My savior.

DON JUAN.

    I am?

ELVIRA.

    Oh I know this is peculiar behavior

    From a woman you hardly know.

DON JUAN.
	We did speak once.
ELVIRA.
	But my heart was too full to say what I mean.
DON JUAN.
	I think it was near the city latrine.
ELVIRA.
	You remember!
DON JUAN.
	I had just walked out of the privy
	Where I was perusing a copy of Livy ...
ELVIRA.
	And I was faint! I was on fire!
DON JUAN.
	Because of the odor?
ELVIRA.
	Because of *desire*.
	Oh, the shame of it!
DON JUAN.
	You were on your horse,
	I can't remember the name of it ...
ELVIRA.
	You're on guard against your passion, I see.
	Oh my angel, you're so much better than me!
	Your soul is like the uppermost apple
	On the highest bough.
DON JUAN.
	May I get up now?
ELVIRA.
	Unreachable. Unimpeachable.
	Can I make it any clearer?
DON JUAN.
	Um.
ELVIRA.
	Don Juan?
DON JUAN.
	Yes, Dona Elvira?

ELVIRA.

I'm pouring out my heart
Yet you don't have much to say.

DON JUAN.

I'm sorry. I guess I just got ...
(Happens to glance at his hand.)
... "carried away."

ELVIRA.

Carried away? Yes, by — ?

DON JUAN.   *(Checks hand.)*

Your beauty?

ELVIRA.

Continuez.

DON JUAN.   *(Reading off of his hand.)*

Well. I lie inert ... all night ... bumming for you.

ELVIRA.

"Inert" and "bumming"?

DON JUAN.

Or alert and beaming.

ELVIRA.

It's possible.

DON JUAN.

Anyway I lie all night tossing and turning.

ELVIRA.   *(Checking his palm for him.)*

Oh. *"Burning."*

DON JUAN.

Yes, burning.

ELVIRA.

For — ?

DON JUAN.

You...?

ELVIRA.

You don't.

DON JUAN.

I do.
(Checks hand.)
"My godless idiot." Or "gormless."

ELVIRA. *(Checks hand.)*
> That is what it looks like.

DON JUAN.
> Sort of formless.

ELVIRA.
> Is that more down here on the wrist?

DON JUAN.
> A birthmark.

ELVIRA.
> No matter. I get the gist.

(Embraces him.)
> Oh my darling, I don't believe it!
> You've declared your love!

DON JUAN.
> I have?

ELVIRA.
> I dreamed it would happen like this!

DON JUAN.
> You did?

ELVIRA.
> What absolute bliss!
> But now maybe it's time for ...

DON JUAN.
> Yes?

ELVIRA.
> "Happen like *this*. Absolute *bliss*. Time for a — "?

DON JUAN.
> Kiss?

ELVIRA.
> My Adonis!

(They kiss, as Leporello enters.)

LEPORELLO.   Hiya, kids! It's only me, the humble prole-
tarian. Don't let me interrupt anything. Just doing the housework, thought I'd air out this old *bed* in here. *(He pulls down
a section of a wall and a canopied Murphy bed folds out of it.)*
Whew! Now how's that for a pleasant stretch of ticking? And
hey — 'case you decide to take the weight off your feet, you
get a taste for satin pillowcases, you be my guest. Well! That's

all the housework I got in here! Quick and easy, huh?
(To audience.)

So whaddya think? Will he get his nozzle off?
(To Don Juan and Elvira.)

Carry on, kids! *Mazel tov!*
(As if leaving, he hides behind the bed.)
ELVIRA.

Well Don Juan, now that you've said that you're
mine …
DON JUAN.

Excuse me, do you have the time?
ELVIRA.

I beg your pardon?
DON JUAN.

Have you got a clock, or a watch of some kind?
ELVIRA.

Really, Don Juan.

DON JUAN.

You know these personal tics.
ELVIRA.

Slightly unromantic, but —
(Checks watch.)

— a quarter to six.
DON JUAN.

Good, we're not running late.
ELVIRA.

Do you have an appointment, or a date — ?
DON JUAN.

No, no, I'm perfectly free.
I'm sorry. Where were we?
ELVIRA.

Declaring our love.
LEPORELLO.

Romance her! Get to the sex!
DON JUAN.

Actually — is it my answer? —
I'm not quite sure what comes next.

ELVIRA.

Well now that you and I have spoken ...

DON JUAN.

Would you like to lie down?

ELVIRA.

Saucy boy! You give me a *token*.

DON JUAN.

Of — ?

ELVIRA.

Our undying love.

DON JUAN.

Sorry. I'm a little dull.

ELVIRA.

Just any old token.

DON JUAN.

I do have a skull.

(Holds it up.)

ELVIRA.

How very kind.

DON JUAN.

Inapropos?

ELVIRA.

Not if it's yours, my beau.

DON JUAN.

Maybe something else.

(Searches further.)

ELVIRA.

A toy or a trifle — any handy thing.

Some family bauble. A *ring* ...

DON JUAN.

There must be something ...

ELVIRA.

My darling, my darling,

You're such a dreamer.

DON JUAN.

What about a nice silver creamer?

ELVIRA.

You know, Don Juan, we're a perfect match.

I speak French and German.

DON JUAN.

English?

ELVIRA.

Natch.

And a smattering of Dutch.

DON JUAN.

(Holds up an astrolabe.)

Do you like this?

ELVIRA.

Not much.

LEPORELLO.

What a geek!

ELVIRA.

Latin and Greek, of course.

Astronomy, philosophy, and the arrow and bow.

DON JUAN.   *(Holds up the hourglass.)*

What about this?

LEPORELLO and ELVIRA.   *(Together.)*

Mmmm. No.

(Don Juan searches again.)

ELVIRA.

Don't worry, darling.

Just something to hold by my heart and keep with me.

DON JUAN.

Listen, if I give you something —

Will you sleep with me?

ELVIRA.

I *beg* your pardon, sir?!

DON JUAN.

Was that a gaff?

LEPORELLO.

Moron.

ELVIRA.

Oh I really have to laugh!

DON JUAN.
    Couldn't we have just a *little* sex?
ELVIRA.
    Señor, it's humiliating! What next?
    To think that I came to your door
    Only to be treated like some contemptible ...
DON JUAN.
    Whore?
LEPORELLO.
    He had to say it.
ELVIRA.
    You wretch!
DON JUAN.
    I'm sorry.
ELVIRA.
    You monster! You worm!
DON JUAN.
    I thought you couldn't think of the term!
ELVIRA.
    The problem, sir, is not my vocabulary.
DON JUAN.
    No need to call out the constabulary.
ELVIRA.
    Oh, I *see.*
LEPORELLO.
    That's right. Confront her.
ELVIRA.
    Now the problem is *me.*
DON JUAN.
    Well isn't it?
LEPORELLO.
    Shame her. Insult her.
DON JUAN.
    But isn't that what you came for? Adultery?
ELVIRA.
    We're not married, we can't commit adultery.

DON JUAN.

    Don't quibble with me.

ELVIRA.

    An impossibility,

    Given your command of the word.

DON JUAN.

    Sophist!

ELVIRA.

    Sophomore!

DON JUAN.

    Temptress!

ELVIRA.

    Turd!

DON JUAN.

    Now I see it! You came here to seduce me!

ELVIRA.

    Villain! How can you reduce me

    To such a base motive?

DON JUAN.

    You didn't come here to light a *votive* ...

    Candle!

LEPORELLO.

    Wonderful.

DON JUAN.

    I swear women were put on earth to test us.

LEPORELLO.

    Oh God, where's my asbestos?

DON JUAN.

    Can you defend your actions?

ELVIRA.

    I can if you'll let me.

LEPORELLO.

    Beelzebub? Come 'n' get me!

DON JUAN.

    Go on. Defend yourself. You can, I trust.

ELVIRA.

    It's true I may have come here with lust

    In my heart ...

DON JUAN.

> HA!

ELVIRA.

> But love was there too, Don Juan.
> Love was the greater part.
> Love — which is the greatest of the arts
> That God, all-seeing,
> Has given us — the natural uninstructed skill
> Of cherishing another human being.
> And I have loved you since the first day
> I saw you at Mass in Seville.
> You were ten and I was eight,
> And since that morning I've done nothing but wait.
> I've turned down suitors, sent back charms,
> Hoping you'd find your way into my arms.
> I lived in hope, that was the sum of it.
> When nothing seemed to come of it,
> I decided to take things into my own hands.
> Oh I can see by your eyes that you don't understand.

DON JUAN.

> I do, I think, if only faintly.

ELVIRA.

> A man so honest *and* so saintly — ?

DON JUAN.

> Women have no outlets.
> They're all repressed by bastards like me.

ELVIRA.

> He comprehends women!
> What a rare joy to see!
> I'm sorry, Don Juan. Goodbye.

(She turns to go.)

DON JUAN.

> Elvira, if you don't sleep with me, I'll die!

(Elvira stops.)

ELVIRA.

> *Pardon?*

DON JUAN.

> For all eternity I'll burn in the fiery pit.

ELVIRA.

Really?

LEPORELLO.

I think he just hit it.

DON JUAN.

I'll languish in an everlasting prison.

Unto ages and ages I'll perish, my —

(Checks his hand.)

— pigeon. My servant will, too.

ELVIRA.

I don't see what he's got to do with it.

DON JUAN.

You know how I cherish you.

ELVIRA.

Not really. Tell me.

DON JUAN.

How could you doubt me?

ELVIRA.

Give me *details*. What do you cherish about me?

DON JUAN.

Well ...

LEPORELLO.

Praise her eyes!

DON JUAN.

There's your size.

ELVIRA.

My *size?*

DON JUAN.

I mean — your eyes.

ELVIRA.

Which I'm told are divine.

DON JUAN.

And then there's your ...

LEPORELLO.

Hair.

DON JUAN.

Your hair, which is ...

ELVIRA.

Top of the line.

DON JUAN.

Your hands? Your skin?

ELVIRA.

I hear they're acceptable.

LEPORELLO.

Your lips.

DON JUAN.

Your hips. Your bodice.

ELVIRA.

Am I detestable?

DON JUAN.

Elvira, you're a goddess!

LEPORELLO.

How you suffer.

DON JUAN.

How I suffer.

LEPORELLO.

You love her!

DON JUAN.

I love her!

ELVIRA.

You love her *who?*

DON JUAN.

Who else —

(Checks his hand.)

— my pet shop — but you?
You pierced my armor
But I didn't know how to tell you.

ELVIRA.

Charmer.

DON JUAN.

But now that I smell you —
I mean, smell your perfume —
And feel you so close ...

ELVIRA.

Resume.

DON JUAN.

    I don't know what to do!

ELVIRA.

    Then to our own selves let's be true.

    We're fated to love and be lovers, my treasure,

    Shouldn't we enjoy the ultimate pleasure

    If the heart is one and the blood is furious?

DON JUAN.

    I am getting rather curious ...

ELVIRA.

    The merging of self at the urge of the flesh,

    The absolute rush, the intimate mesh?

DON JUAN.

    Yesh! Yesh! Yesh!

ELVIRA.

    We'll join soul to soul, body to body, head to head.

    And there's only place to do that, my darling.

DON JUAN.

    Where's that? You mean...?

LEPORELLO.

    Bed!

DON JUAN.

    Bed?

ELVIRA.

    Bed.

(Don Juan and Elvira get into bed. Leporello steps forward and addresses the audience as he draws the bed-curtains.)

LEPORELLO. *(To audience.)* That's enough, that's enough! Pardon me, while I veil this tender scene from view. We got a contingent of theatrical voyeurs here, these guys who buy front-row seats for the astronomical view of the ladies. I'm talking to *you,* sicko. Well! So the kid finally scored, huh. Saved our asses for a day. Now all he has to do is repeat this a trillion times. Wow. That is a lot of action. Could wear out his dong and put him in traction. But let's check up on our busy hero. *(Peeks inside the curtains.)* Copulation, one. Eternal truth, zero. Wuh-oh. Hang on now. Steady.

DON JUAN. *(Orgasm, behind the curtain.)* Veni! *Vidi! VICI!*

LEPORELLO. Sounds like they're finished. The Don is done already...? *(Don Juan appears from the bed looking bedraggled.)*
DON JUAN. So that was sex. Huh...!
LEPORELLO. And what's the verdict on this filthy act, my winsome gigolo?
DON JUAN. Scientifically? I think ... *(Considers.)* ... that might be worth a second try. *(He starts back for the bed, but —.)*
LEPORELLO. Hold it, hold it! You can't, remember?
DON JUAN. What?
LEPORELLO. The contract.
DON JUAN. Oh, right. That's ... unfortunate.
LEPORELLO. You done her now she's off the list.
DON JUAN.

> But Leporello, when I embraced her my heart leapt up.

LEPORELLO.

> Not the only organ your blood kept up.

DON JUAN.

> No, no! This was some cosmic nexus! Ineffable!

LEPORELLO.

> But in your case, your ex's aren't eff-able.

ELVIRA. *(From the bed.)*

> Don Juan?

LEPORELLO.

> I'm gone. *(Leporello hides behind the bed again.)*

ELVIRA.

> Don Juan? Hello?

(Looks out from the bed.)

> Hey there lover, where'd you go?

DON JUAN.

> I'm sorry. Is there more?

ELVIRA.

> More?

DON JUAN.

> I mean wasn't that enough?

ELVIRA.

> That? Enough?

LEPORELLO.
> Seatbelts, folks. This could get rough.

DON JUAN.
> Somehow I thought that we were done.

ELVIRA.
> In a manner of speaking. I lost. You won.

DON JUAN.
> Amazing how short a time it took.
>
> But I was going to go back to my —

ELVIRA.
> — book?

(Slams it shut.)
> How dare you, sir!

DON JUAN.
> You seem to be upset.

ELVIRA.
> I bare to you my body and this is what I get?
>
> Didn't you pledge your love?
>
> Offer me a token?

DON JUAN.
> The problem is — my dove —
>
> I'm already bespoken.

ELVIRA.
> You mean there's another woman?

DON JUAN.
> No.

ELVIRA.
> Not a *man?*

DON JUAN.
> A spirit.

ELVIRA.
> Explain this, if you can.

DON JUAN.
> Well I can't. Not easily.

ELVIRA.
> Oh *please.* Now that we're off your convenient couch.
>
> Go on.

DON JUAN.

The long and short of it —

ELVIRA.

I've had the short. Give me the long.

LEPORELLO.

Ouch!

DON JUAN.

We can't do this ever again.

I know it was wrong —

ELVIRA.

Wrong? To take advantage of me that way?

DON JUAN.

I wish I could explain, my Venus.

ELVIRA.

Walking penises, that's all men are!

DON JUAN.

The fact is, I have to take a very long trip.

Leporello! Pack my grip!

(He starts out, she holds him back.)

ELVIRA.

Didn't you mean all those things you said?

DON JUAN.

Every word!

ELVIRA.

I see. Before we hit the bed.

DON JUAN.

I do apologize for causing you pain.

ELVIRA.

And yet —

DON JUAN.

And yet I have this other obligation

That I can't explain.

ELVIRA.

Oh. "Obligation." That's good.

DON JUAN.

Which I'd undo if I could.

ELVIRA.

Tell me a new one, Don Joo-un.

DON JUAN.

    Elvira,

    In matters of the heart I'm a mere apprentice.

ELVIRA.

    The way you're hurting me, you're more of a —

DON JUAN.

    Dentist,

    I know. But you know about love, and the human
        body.

    I'm a clod. You have the touch of a surgeon.

ELVIRA.

    Don Juan, until this day — I was a virgin.

DON JUAN.

    Somehow I thought your experiences

    Had been very ... varied.

ELVIRA.

    I had no experience.

    So in the eyes of God, we're very married.

DON JUAN.

    I'm sorry that this wasn't all you wanted it to be.

    But blame that on blundering youth,

    Not some lack of affection in me.

    I even see dimly that, in some other life,

    You and I might have been —

ELVIRA.

    Man and wife.

DON JUAN.

    But we can't be.

ELVIRA.

    That's your word?

DON JUAN.

    I've spoken.

ELVIRA.

    My lord, I gave you my heart and now it's broken.

    All these years there was the great Don Juan.

    Noble. Gracious. A *sine qua non*.

    The thought of nothing, not even of myself,

    Was dearer to me than you.

DON JUAN.

Elvira, I can only say I'm deeply grieved.

Now with your permission,

Though not your comprehension,

I'll take my leave. *Adieu.*

Forgive me.

(He kisses her hand and starts out.)

ELVIRA.

You won't explain? Or even try?

DON JUAN.

Actually ...

LEPORELLO.

Ixnay, sire. Let's fly. *(Don Juan and Leporello exit.)*

ELVIRA.

Ravished and abandoned! Scorned and smeared!

Behold. Vulgar tears

Where none had flowed before this.

And am I, Dona Maria Elvira de Flores,

To be degraded by this oaf, this ox,

Who turns the key and then discards the box?

No, as God is my witness, by this hand,

I will not rest until I have that man!

Listen to me, you stars! Hear what I tell you!

(Suddenly, in a puff of smoke, Mephistopheles appears.)

MEPHISTOPHELES.

Good evening. *(Cough.)* Maybe I can help you.

ELVIRA.

Who are you? A spirit? From what region?

Don't tell me. Is your name — ?

MEPHISTOPHELES.

— Legion. It's true.

ELVIRA.

A devil, but coughing?

MEPHISTOPHELES.

I can't explain it. Can you?

ELVIRA.

What do you want, Satan?

MEPHISTOPHELES.

Dona Elvira, I'm nothing if not pliant,

And though you never seemed a likely client,

Still, Don Juan ...

ELVIRA.

Don't say that name, please, don't go on.

Yes? Don Juan?

MEPHISTOPHELES.

I see how much you love the Don.

I can see it by your tears.

ELVIRA.

I've simply waited for so many years.

This is a love that was fated to be.

MEPHISTOPHELES.

Love's a total mystery to *me*.

ELVIRA.

That man is like a fire burning inside of me.

MEPHISTOPHELES.

Well you know the old adage:

It's not the fire, it's the water damage.

(Magically produces a handkerchief.)

ELVIRA.

Did you just make that up?

MEPHISTOPHELES.

I do confess.

ELVIRA.

You're a clever devil.

MEPHISTOPHELES.

I *am* a clever devil, yes.

ELVIRA.

Now on the level, what do you want with me?

MEPHISTOPHELES.

To help you to the Don.

ELVIRA.

Oh God — just to make love with him

Once more before my final hour chimes!

MEPHISTOPHELES.

To catch him, you'd need a good long time.

ELVIRA.

But how? I'm cursed!

I could die first!

And then where would I be?

MEPHISTOPHELES. *(Producing a contract.)*

Why don't you look at Paragraph Three.

ELVIRA. *(Reads.)*

"Dona Elvira ..."

MEPHISTOPHELES.

"Shall never die ..."

ELVIRA.

"Till she and Don Juan ..."

MEPHISTOPHELES.

"A second time together lie."

It's quite simple. If you want a chance at him ...

ELVIRA.

A chance to dance in revenge on him. The slime.

To grind in my heel!

MEPHISTOPHELES.

Then the solution, my dear, is sublime.

(Holds out the quill pen.)

Let's make a deal.

END OF ACT ONE

ACT TWO

Chicago

The present. Evening.

The clock strikes six as lights come up on Don Juan's apartment. It looks much like his chamber in Seville, but with doorways to the rest of the apartment at left and right. Where the alchemical equipment had been is a bar. The hourglass is on a shelf, the skull is on a desk, the astrolabe is in a corner. A shabby couch, center. The wall of books has been replaced by a wall of black-bound books.

The door to the outside opens. Don enters in a shabby lounge-lizard outfit and shades, with Sandy, 40, a chain-smoking corporate exec. Don turns the lights on.

DON. Well. This is the place. It's not exactly a castle in Spain.

SANDY. No, I wouldn't call it a castle in Spain. Maybe a dump on the south side of Chicago. *(Picks up a pair of lacy panties from the couch.)* Very pretty. Yours?

DON. Ah. My dust rag. Thank you. *(Quickly disposes of the panties.)* Anyway — welcome. Put your feet up. Lie down. Or whatever your ... inclination is.

SANDY. What do you pay for this?

DON. Eighty dollars a month.

SANDY. You're kidding. When did you move in?

DON. Forty-three years ago.

SANDY. Oh. A sense of humor. I like that. *(The skull.)* Ashtray?

DON. Skull, actually. *(Sandy flicks her ashes into the eyehole of the skull. He moves in on her. She holds him off.)*

SANDY. One second, Dick.

DON. It's Don, actually.

SANDY. Don Jackson?

DON. Don Johnson.

SANDY. I ought to tell you, I don't do this every day.

DON. You mean visit a gentleman's apartment for some light refreshment, my dove?

SANDY. No, I mean pick up a stranger at a bar for uninhibited fucking.

DON. So think of this as a return to more carefree days. And here I am. The perfect stranger. *(They kiss.)*

SANDY. Your phone light is blinking.

DON. Ah. Thank you. *(Don hits a button on the phone machine.)*

WOMAN'S VOICE ON PHONE MACHINE. This is your "date" from last night, you vampire! You prick! You suck the blood of women and then you throw their lifeless bodies away — *(Don turns it off.)*

DON. Wrong number, I guess.

SANDY. Uh-huh.

DON. But can I take your wrap, Wendy?

SANDY. Excuse me?

DON. Help you with your coat? — Is something wrong, Wendy?

SANDY. Sandy.

DON. I'm sorry. That bar was pretty loud. There was a lot of shouting going on.

SANDY. Are you saying I was shouting?

DON. Actually you were shouting.

SANDY. I believe my boyfriend was shouting, was he not?

DON. Oh. Was that your boyfriend?

SANDY. Don't get me started on *him.*

DON. All right.

SANDY. Don't get me started on Todd the rat.

DON. Okay.

SANDY. Todd the *vermin.*

DON. Take your coat?

SANDY. Thanks, Lancelot. I think I know how to take a coat

off. *(She takes it off and dumps it in his hands.)*
DON.   Absolutely. Lefty! — My butler. — *Lefty! (Leporello appears in ancient tattered livery.)*
LEPORELLO.   *What.*
DON.   We have a guest.
LEPORELLO.   Ah. *Zooom befehl, mein Kommandant! ["Zum befehl": at your command.]*
DON.   Take the lady's coat, please.
LEPORELLO.   *Prado, signore.* And what a lovely, lyrical lady it is!
DON.   Would you excuse me, Wendy?
SANDY.   Sandy.
DON.   Sandy. *(Aside to Leporello.)* Bad news, Leporello.
LEPORELLO.   Do tell.
DON.   I-ay ink-thay I-ay aw-say *Er*-hay oo-tay ight-nay.
LEPORELLO.   Utt-way the *uck*-fay are you talking about?
DON.   I think I saw Elvira tonight.
LEPORELLO.   Help me, God, help me, help me!
DON.   At the bar, disguised as a cocktail waitress.
LEPORELLO.   We lost her. In Mexico City, in '49.
DON.   We lost her in Dusseldorf in '28, Calcutta in '22 ...
LEPORELLO.   I'll check the apartment. *(Leporello goes out.)*
DON.   So — something wrong?
SANDY.   Question, Dick.
DON.   It's Don, actually.
SANDY.   If I wasn't here right now, you and your so-called "butler" wouldn't be on the rug here fondling each other, now would you?
DON.   Lefty and me? No, I let Lefty fondle himself. In private, of course.
    But let me ask, without much reason
    though with rhyme,
    would you happen to have —
SANDY.   A watch?
DON.
    — the time?
SANDY.   I think you have a watch right there on your wrist.
DON.   I always have this nagging pathological fear that it's

stopped on me.

SANDY.   And a clock up there on the wall.

DON.   It could be slow.

SANDY.   A little therapy might speed it up. — Six twenty-two.

DON.   Excellent.

SANDY.   Do you have an appointment somewhere?

DON.   No no no no, I'm all yours tonight. And vice versa, I hope. *(He moves in, she holds him off.)*

SANDY.   Some ground rules. You're not "into" anything, are you? I mean, nipple pins, neck chains, cock locks, butt plugs, golden showers, B-and-D, S-and-M, any other acronymic perversion?

DON.   My only kink is copulation.

SANDY.   I refuse to strap on a dildo.

DON.   Deal.

SANDY.   Twice in a lifetime is enough.

DON.

But here's a happy bit of happenstance.
An album called "A Night of Soft Romance."
Would you care for a foxtrot? Shall we dance?

(He kisses her neck. There's knock at the door.) Would you excuse me for a second? *(He opens the door to Mike, 23, hunkish and personable.)*

MIKE.   Don. Hi. Mike, from 9A — ?

DON.   Yes. Hi. Mike.... What's up?

MIKE.   Well I see you got company, I was just hoping maybe you could help me out with a little personal problem. But that's okay.

DON.   I am sort of tied up right now ...

MIKE.   No, no, no, that's okay, sorry to butt in like this.

DON.   Maybe another time.

MIKE.   Absolutely. Anytime. No problem.

DON.   'Bye! *(Shuts the door.)* So. Can I offer you a soothing libation?

SANDY.   Red wine, no sulfites.

DON.   Your wish is my demand. *(Leporello enters.)* Lefty?

LEPORELLO.   All clear.

DON. *Vino rosso per due.*

LEPORELLO. *Instamatico, signore. (He pours wine.)*

DON. So tell me about yourself.... Um. Tell me.

SANDY. Well. My name is still Sandy. Two: I don't sleep around with just anybody. However. Three: Tonight happens to be a very peculiar night.

DON. Ah-ha.

SANDY. As I happen to be going through something rather painful at the moment.

DON. I see.

SANDY. *Extremely* painful, in fact.

DON. I'm sorry.

SANDY. You're not going to ask *why* this is a particularly painful night?

DON. It couldn't be your boyfriend...?

SANDY. Oh you mean Todd the *rat?* Todd the *VERMIN?* Why should it be painful that my rodent boyfriend rolls over in his sleep, puts his hand on my tit and says, *"Blow me again, Tiffany"* — ? *(Leporello brings them wine glasses.)*

DON. Well, cheers.

SANDY. Why should it be painful that I discover this asshole has also slept, during our time together, with a Kimberley, a Heather, a Joy, and Imelda my cleaning lady?

DON. So you've been together a long time?

SANDY. Five weeks.

DON. Chin-chin.

SANDY. You know why I date guys like this? It's my mother. She starved me with her emotional distance so now, if any man says he likes me, I'm a sucker.

DON. *I* like you.

SANDY. Do you really?

DON. Very much. Skol.

SANDY. Or it could be my father.

DON. He starved you?

SANDY. No. He died.

DON. I'm sorry.

SANDY. I'm sixteen years old, I get knocked up by some nickel-and-dime Don Juan passing through town.... Hey. You haven't ever been in Illyria, Illinois, have you? Say, 23 years ago?

DON.   Illyria, Illinois? Um, no, doesn't ring a bell …

SANDY.   I should hope not. *(Leporello sneaks into the room and goes to the shelves of black books.)*

LEPORELLO.   Illyria, Illinois, 23 years ago … *(He starts checking one of the black books.)*

SANDY.   I tell my father I'm pregnant, and *bang*, he drops dead of a heart attack. Not a great man, but the only father I had. And you know what? I still think of him every day. And this baby I abandoned. My little daughter. I'm sorry …

DON.   Look. You're going through a lot right now. We don't have to do this. *(His watch beeps.)* Actually, yes we do.

SANDY.   You're goddamn right we do. I'm gonna get revenge on Todd *and* on my father *and* on the bastard who knocked me up all at one time.

DON.   Very economical.

SANDY.   You are my weapon, Dick.

DON.   Don, actually.

SANDY.   I hope you have condoms.

DON.   *(Producing a roll of them.)* Better latex than never.

SANDY.   The membrane of the wedding. Doctor's certificate? *(Don shows one.)* Blood test? *(Don shows it.)* Sexual history? *(He just looks at the wall of black books.)* I hope I'm over this yeast infection … *(She lies down on the couch.)*

DON.   You know, Keats once read me a wonderful — once wrote a wonderful poem about love …

SANDY.   Why are we discussing literature? I thought we were having sex.

DON.   Yes, let's have sex by all means.

SANDY.   Wouldn't you like to unbutton this two-hundred-dollar blouse?

DON.   Gladly.

SANDY.   *(Pulling back.)* What do you say?

DON.   "Please"?

SANDY.   Go for it. *(Don starts unbuttoning her blouse, but Leporello steps in.)*

LEPORELLO.   Cool it, Donny. You slept with this one already.

DON.   I what?

LEPORELLO.   She's in the black book. Volume 246. *(Don gets up off the couch.)*

DON.   Uhhhhhhh Sandy, I'm afraid I'm going to have to ask you to leave.

SANDY.   What do you mean, leave?

DON.   Coat, please.

SANDY.   Hey! Cunnilingus was in the air!

DON.   The fact is, I have to take a very long trip.

LEPORELLO.   *Very* long trip.

SANDY.   What are you talking about?

DON.   *(Holding out her coat.)* I'm very sorry.

LEPORELLO.   Deepest apologies.

DON.   Maybe we can meet for a cup of coffee sometime.

LEPORELLO.   When we get back.

DON.   When I get back.

SANDY.   Bastard!

DON.   I'm very sorry but you have to leave.

SANDY.   I don't believe this! *(Knock at door.)* Who's *this,* now? The next girl in line for you to arouse and abandon at your Gothic fuck-pad?

DON.   I don't know who this is. *(Another knock.)*

TODD.   *(Offstage.)* Sandy! Sandy? Are you there?

SANDY.   Oh. It's Todd.

DON.   Todd?

SANDY.   The rat!

TODD.   *(Offstage.)* Sandy, I know you're in there! Let me in!

DON.   You're going to have to leave now.

SANDY.   Let him in.

DON.   Sandy, you have to leave!

SANDY.   I'm glad you finally learned my name. I said let him in! I'll show that bastard I can have a *fling.*

DON.   If I let him in, will you leave?

SANDY.   Tell him we've been fucking our brains out.

DON.   If I tell him, will you leave?

SANDY. Just let him in.

TODD. *(Offstage.)* Sandy! Open up!

SANDY. I said let him in!

DON. Okay ... *(Don opens the door and Todd enters: 40 and a suit.)* Hello, Todd.

SANDY. You RAT.

TODD. Sandy, come with me.

SANDY. So you found me.

TODD. I followed you here from that disgusting bar.

SANDY. Maybe the same place you met *Imelda*.

TODD. Will you come with me before it's too late?

SANDY. Sorry, Todd. I have just fucked this man into a total sexual stupor.

TODD. Will you come with me, please?

SANDY. Tell him, Dick.

DON. I am in a total sexual stupor.

TODD. I want you to come back to my place and we'll discuss this in rational fashion.

SANDY. How many orgasms have I had?

DON. Does anybody have the time?

SANDY. I bet I've had a hundred orgasms tonight. Which is ninety-three more than *you* ever gave me.

TODD. I didn't come here for a head count.

SANDY. This man has a pikestaff. This man has *cojones*.

DON. Could you two leave, please?

SANDY. So how do you feel now, Mr. Fuckover?

TODD. You know what this is, don't you? This is your sister.

SANDY. No, this is not my sister, this is your mother.

TODD. Can we not bring my mother into this?

SANDY. And what she did with the soup spoon?

TODD. If anything it's the incident with my brother when I was five. Oh GOD, OH GOD! I'M REMEMBERING IT!

DON. If you two want to stay here and have a session, I have to go out.

TODD. Sit down, asshole.

DON. MOVE IT, TODD! *(He moves toward Todd, but Todd puts the point of his umbrella up to Don's chest.)*

TODD. Make me. *(Don grabs an umbrella from an umbrella stand.*

Todd thrusts, Don parries, and in a moment we're watching a regulation sword fight that moves up and over the couch and around the room. During the fight, Todd loses his glasses. As they fight.)

SANDY. Oh sure. Fine. Penis substitutes. That's all men ever know. Phallic Objects and How To Manipulate Them. Well I don't have to stand here and watch this crypto-homoerotic love-play. If you want me, you worm, I'll be at home revving up the vibrator, getting more affection from General Electric than *you* ever gave me. *(Suddenly Sandy stops.)* Wait a minute. WAIT A MINUTE. *FREEZE! (Don and Todd freeze.)* What is that?

DON. It's an astrolabe.

SANDY. And your name is Dick Jackson?

DON. *Don Johnson.*

TODD. Bastard.

SANDY. Todd, that's him.

TODD. That's who.

SANDY. That's him. That's the father of my baby!

DON. I'm the what?

SANDY. *That's the man who killed my father!*

DON. I'm the what?!

SANDY. *That's Don JOHNSON!*

DON. *Dick* Johnson, actually. Jackson.

SANDY. And the bastard looks younger than me! Kill him, Todd.

TODD. What...?

SANDY. Kill him.

TODD. I can't kill him. I can't even see him. Have you seen my glasses?

SANDY. Take that man's life and I'm yours forever. *KILL HIM! KILL HIM! KILL HIM! (Leporello has opened the door.)*

LEPORELLO. Donny, go! *(Don runs out and Leporello blocks the door.)*

SANDY. Get out of my way.

LEPORELLO. Look, don't take this so personally!

SANDY. I said GET OUT OF MY WAY! *(She runs out, followed by Todd.)*

TODD. *Sandy? Sandy! We have to talk! (The clock strikes seven.)*

LEPORELLO. *(To us.)* Modern life and welcome to it. Four

hundred years of this shit, can you imagine? Feels like a thousand, but who's counting. I mean, life kinda flattens out once you pass the big four-oh-oh. And lose all your dough. Yeah, spring of 1896, Mr. Rocket Scientist invests the family fortune in this new invention called the automobile. Great idea, except he bought a hundred thousand shares of the Sam Berkowitz Auto Company. Straight into the toilet. And Allison the milkmaid? Yeah, well, didn't work out, one thing and another. Immortality and so on. I'm circumnavigating the globe and she marries the town butcher. Milkmaid. Butcher. Nice balanced diet. I'd blow into town every now and again, and there's Allison getting older and older and me getting samer and samer. The lines showing up on her face, the hair goes grey — still beautiful as the first day I met her. Yeah. Sweet Allison the udderly wonderful milkmaid. Had five kids and nineteen grandchildren. Died in the summer of 1651, sitting on a chair out in front of her house, peeling potatoes. 68 years old. *(Don comes in through the window.)* Comes the Don.
DON.   Are they gone?
LEPORELLO.   You do know how to pick 'em, my prince. *(Don collapses on the couch.)*
DON.   Oh, God ...
LEPORELLO.   Hey, don't you collapse on me. You gotta go back out there and get laid.
DON.   Not *again*. Not *again*.
LEPORELLO.   *Auf geht's*, Romeo. *Arriba!*
DON.   I still have time.
LEPORELLO.   Oh yeah? You went out to find *this* cookie at ten this morning.
DON.   Look, don't tell me my job. I am the *Don*, remember?
LEPORELLO.   Do you want to die?
DON.   Yes I do.
LEPORELLO.   No you do *not*. And get that shirt off, you look like a dog's dessert.
DON.   Another day, another Dolores ... *(He takes off his jacket and Leporello gives him a tie.)*
LEPORELLO.   Put this on. I give you two minutes to freshen up, Sweetie.

DON. *(To us.)*
> Behold my situation, and ponder it.
> I get immortality — and squander it,
> Pouring scotch and wrestling pantyhose.
> I have spent my life checking my watch
> And taking off my clothes.
> As for the meaning of life,
> Who's had time to look?
> Since Tolstoy died I haven't cracked a book.
> My life's a shell, content-free.
> Hold me to your ear and you could hear the sea.

Lefty.

LEPORELLO. *("Your Highness.")* Your Anus?

DON. I am completely out of place in this benighted age.

LEPORELLO. Actually, you were pretty weird for 1590. Speaking of which, can I get a raise, please? Since I'm still making two doubloons per annum?

DON. The first age in history when celibacy is a blessing and it's the only thing that can kill me.

LEPORELLO. Oh, are you gonna tell *me* about celibacy? I been so busy holding down two jobs and keeping you in the saddle, I haven't gotten laid since the Crimean *War*. So bitch to me.

DON. You're the one who egged me on in the first place. "Genital stimulation! Genital stimulation!"

LEPORELLO. This is ancient history, okay? Just pardon me for all those pesky hard-ons you been having.

DON. I don't do this because I *like* it, you know.

LEPORELLO. Oh. Excuse me.

DON. Sex is not fun. Sex is my *job*. You don't have to get an erection seven days a week, 365 days a year. Decade in, decade out.

LEPORELLO. What's an erection?

DON. Eternity in hell looks like a beach in Tahiti compared to this. Compared to "Hi, I'm Don, I love pasta Alfredo and I think Steinfeld is a genius."

LEPORELLO. *Seinfeld*, you idiot.

DON.   Four centuries and what have I done?

LEPORELLO.   A million laps in the dating pool.

DON.   Johnny Keats lived for 25 years and his poetry will be remembered for all time. I'll be forgotten the minute I'm gone.

LEPORELLO.   Hey, hey. None of that "moment-I'm-gone" shit. We go on, remember? We go on. Speaking of which, did I hear the name "Keats" wafting through the room tonight?

DON.   What's wrong with Keats?

LEPORELLO.   Keats is no longer a viable come-on, Candide.

DON.   Keats was a great romantic poet.

LEPORELLO.   Wonderful.

DON.   And a close personal friend.

LEPORELLO.   Terrific. Call up Keats and sleep with *him*. Only you better do it by midnight!

DON.   Listen, Caliban. I wrote the book on seduction.

DON and LEPORELLO.   *(Together.) I am the Don!*

DON.   Where's the woman who'd give Keats the time of day these days? He'd be reciting the Ode on a Grecian Urn and she'd be quoting "Star Trek."

LEPORELLO.   Well look at the debs you been hanging out with! Not the first place to go for new insights into Nietzsche.

DON.   And now I'm a father...? If that poor woman was right, I'm a father! My God. I have a daughter!

LEPORELLO.   Listen, Spermbank. The way you been copulating, you coulda been populating China.

DON.   Where is this heir to the noble name of Tenorio y Saavedra?

LEPORELLO.   What're you gonna do, launch into Rogers and Hammerstein? You gotta walk the shlong, Cinderella, or we turn into pumpkin pie.

DON.   I'm a father...!

LEPORELLO.   *Gosh, look, Dad! It's seven-thirty!*

DON.   And I abandoned her. *(Knock at door.)*

LEPORELLO.   It is the fucking Bates Motel around here. *(Leporello opens the door.)*

MIKE.   Lefty, hi.

LEPORELLO.   What's up, Mike?

MIKE.   Well I was wondering if I could talk to Don about a personal question.

LEPORELLO.   We're kinda busy right now trying to stay immortal.

MIKE.   Oh sure. Maybe another time. No problem. *(Leporello shuts the door.)*

LEPORELLO.   Are you ready, your Thickness?

DON.   Ready.

DON and LEPORELLO.   *Bonzai! (They start out. Don stops.)*

DON.   What if we run into Elvira?

LEPORELLO.   Will you get *off* El-Virus? We lost her, okay?

DON.   What if we didn't? What if she tries to trick me into having sex with her?

LEPORELLO.   Two simple words: *Don't.* And I'll tell you why in one word: because you *can't.*

DON.   She doesn't know that.

LEPORELLO.   So put the word out on the Internet. Personally I think you were hallucinating tonight.

DON.   What kind of a deal do you think she cut?

LEPORELLO.   Donny, will you trust me? That woman will *never, ever* — not in a million years — it is IMPOSSIBLE Elvira could ever track us down! *(There is a knock at the door. Don opens it.)*

DON.   Yes? *(Elvira enters, disguised, in a sexy outfit and shades and using a Southern accent.)*

ELVIRA.
> Kind sir, I apologize for bothering you
> And knocking at your door.
> I'm looking for apartment 9W.
> Would that be on this floor?

(Don and Leporello exchange a glance.)

DON and LEPORELLO.
> Nine-double-you …

DON.
> Would you care to *entrer?*

ELVIRA.
> Why thank you, sir. I'm *enchanteé.*
> But really, gentlemen, I don't want to intrude.

DON.

    No, we were just sitting here.

LEPORELLO.

    Watching some tube.

    An homage to Charles Bronson.

DON.

    How do you do. I'm Don Johnson.

ELVIRA.

    I'm Veronica.

DON.

    And my butler, Lefty.

DON, LEPORELLO and ELVIRA.

    How do you do!

DON.

    And what a pleasure it is to meet you, my dear.

(Kisses her hand.)

ELVIRA.   *(To audience.)*

    Actually, it's me again.

(Lifts her shades.)

    Dona El-*veer?*

(To Don and Leporello.)

    Anyway, I don't understand this address.

DON.

    I think the letters only go up to S.

ELVIRA.

    Then I guess this guy was putting me on,

    If it's true what you say, ah —

DON and ELVIRA.

    Don.

ELVIRA.

    So here I am, all dressed up, and stood up.

(Don motions Leporello to leave.)

LEPORELLO.

    Well, guess I'll go put the old hood up.

    G'night!

DON.

    Sweet dreams!

ELVIRA.

　　Don't let the bedbugs bite!

(Leporello exits, flashing a thumbs-up to Don.)

　　I hope I didn't scare off your friend.

DON.

　　Oh no, he had quite a few things to attend ...

　　To.... Excuse me, but —

　　Have I ever seen you somewhere before?

ELVIRA.

　　I never saw you in my life

　　Till I walked through that door.

DON.

　　Must be my imagination.

ELVIRA.

　　I don't take it amiss.

DON.

　　Can I offer you something, Miss Veronica...?

ELVIRA.

　　Bliss.

　　But what a tragedy.

　　I mean, my first hot date in the great big city.

　　I buy a whole new dress. Isn't it pretty?

DON.

　　Mmm. *Yes.*

ELVIRA.

　　Do you like it? Or is it too long?

DON.

　　You could hike it an inch. But I might be wrong.

(The phone rings and the machine picks up.)

SANDY'S VOICE ON PHONE MACHINE.　　This is Sandy, you vampire! You prick! You suck the blood of women and then you throw their lifeless bodies away — *(Don leaps to the phone machine and turns it off.)*

DON.

　　Wrong number, I guess.

ELVIRA.

　　Now that was kinda strange.

64

DON.

City life, huh.

ELVIRA.

Prob'ly deranged.

DON.

But would you care for a cocktail?
A beverage on ice?

ELVIRA.

A glass of red wine would be awfully nice.

DON.

Your wish, Miss Bliss, is my demand.

ELVIRA.

Oh I do love to meet a gentlemanly man!

DON.

House red?

ELVIRA.

You really are kind, sir.

DON.

Do you have the time?

ELVIRA.

Just seven thirty-nine, sir.

DON.

Excellent.

(Knocking at door L.)

Would you excuse me?

ELVIRA.

I would absolutely.

(Don opens the door, and Todd is standing there.)

TODD.   All right, where is she? If you're hiding her, I'll kill you.

DON.   She's not here, Todd.

TODD.   Have you seen her?

DON.   No.

TODD.   Have you seen my glasses?

DON.   No!

TODD.   If you're hiding my glasses, I can sue you for holding stolen property —

DON.   Good night, Todd! *(He shuts the door.)*
ELVIRA.
>Now that was kinda odd.
DON.
>Must be the moon.
ELVIRA.
>This city sure is chockful o' loons.

(Another knock at door.)
DON.   Go away, Todd! *(The door opens to reveal Mike.)*
MIKE.   Actually, it's Mike again. Hello! Sorry! 'Bye! *(Mike closes the door.)*
DON.
>But shall we utilize the sofa?
ELVIRA.
>Mr. Johnson, I hope you don't think I'm a loafer
>But would it be all right if I ... reclined?
DON.
>Miss Bliss, the way you look tonight,
>How could I possibly mind?

(Elvira lies down in a sexy pose.)
ELVIRA.
>Oh yes. Mm-hm. This is infinitely better.
>But now where would *you* like to set?

(Don starts to move alongside her, but pulls back.)
DON.
>Are you *sure* we've never met?
ELVIRA.
>Girl Scout's honor. Want to bet?
DON.
>Maybe in Paris? Common Eurail passes?
>And wouldn't you like to take off those glasses?
ELVIRA.
>Oh no. I couldn't.
DON.
>You'd be more at ease.
ELVIRA.
>But you see I have this terrible optic disease.

I take these off, everything kinda turns into stone.
Something to do with the rods and the cones?

DON.

Veronica, would you excuse me for a second?

ELVIRA.

For a single solitary tick, I reckon.

DON.

And you said your name was —

ELVIRA.

Bliss.

DON.

(Takes a black book off the shelf.)
Bliss. Bliss ...

ELVIRA.

You do what you need to, I'll just keep on talking.
Oh darn it!

DON.

A problem?

ELVIRA.

A run in my stocking.
Will you look at that ladder?
These nylons were new!

DON.

Maybe there's something *I* could do...?

ELVIRA.

Well Mr. Johnson, I know you're a total stranger,
But would you mind if I changed here?
Revitalized this one drooping hose?
Would that shock or offend?

DON.

No! Think of me as a doctor, or friend.

ELVIRA.

Now I know I sound like a martyr,
But this happens to be a particularly sticky garter ...

DON.

I have some digital expertise.
May I assist?

ELVIRA.

Oh *please.*

(They're getting closer and closer, nearing a kiss.)

Unless there's someplace else you need to be ...

DON.

Tonight, Miss Bliss, I am totally free.

ELVIRA.

Total freedom. What a pleasant curse.

DON.

What can I do?

ELVIRA.

Just reach down deep in my velvet purse.

(Don moves in to kiss her, but pulls back.)

DON.

That's funny.

ELVIRA.

A problem?

DON.

We're talking in verse.

That's very odd.

ELVIRA.

Maybe an inspiration from God.

(She draws him back.)

Because you know what rhymes with "bliss,"
Don't you, Don Johnson...?

DON.

Where are you from, Veronica?

ELVIRA.

Me? I'm from Wisconsin.

DON.

And I've never seen you before today?

ELVIRA.

Spent my whole life on a farm, pitching hay.
Playin' the harmonica.

DON.

You don't *sound* like Wisconsin.
More like Kentucky.

ELVIRA.

Well my family's from southern Milwaukee.

The northern flank of the southern tier.

DON.

Uh-huh.

ELVIRA.

Is it getting kinda warm in here?

(She snaps open a Spanish fan.)

DON.

Goddamit, Elvira, this is inhuman!

ELVIRA.

"Elvira ..."?

DON.

You can drop the act.

ELVIRA.

All right it's me.

So how've *you* been?

DON.

Get out of here, Elvira.

ELVIRA.

Don Juan, you've made my life into a river of tears.

DON.

So you've been telling me for *four hundred years.*

Will you ever free me?

ELVIRA.

Aren't you just a little glad to see me?

DON.

Pest! *Cucaracha!*

ELVIRA.

Guess not.

DON.

Can't you give it a rest?

ELVIRA.

Can I help it if I love you?

Is that a crime?

DON.

We *ended,* muchacha! In 1599!

ELVIRA.

> Yes, June 28, the day we began!
> But you won't escape. I have a plan.
> There's our story. I love, you laugh.

DON.

> I wasn't laughing.

ELVIRA.

> Not half.

DON.

> Look, I can appreciate that you're bitter.

ELVIRA.

> Bitter! Oh you're such a *man!*
> Treating all women like kitty litter.

DON.

> Do you have the time?

ELVIRA.

> Why do you hate me? What have I done?

DON.

> I don't hate you. I swear.

ELVIRA.

> Slime.
> Am I so repulsive?

DON.

> *Au contraire,*
> You remain the epitome of pulchritude.

ELVIRA.

> Then what's one more poke to you,
> Who've poked a multitude?
> Just make love to me once.

DON.

> No.

ELVIRA.

> Please.

DON.

> I will not make love to you.

ELVIRA.

> I admit, after four centuries it's a bit sticky.

DON.

     I have to go.

ELVIRA.

     Come on, Don Juan. Just a quickie?

DON.

     No! Never! Goodbye!

(He starts out.)

ELVIRA.

     Don Juan, if you sleep with me — I die.

(Don stops at the door.)

DON.

     Pardon...?

ELVIRA.

     Just love me and you'll be rid of me.

DON.

     Did you say...?

ELVIRA.

     Die. How's that for levity.

DON.

     Die...? How?

ELVIRA.

     You know how I adored you.

DON.

     Yes.

ELVIRA.

     I sold my soul to Satan for you.

DON.

     I knew it couldn't be longevity.

     But this is a lie.

ELVIRA.

     This is a fact.

DON.

     A fabrication to embarrass me.

ELVIRA.

     It's in the contract.

(She produces it.)

     Paragraph Three.

DON.

     You kept your copy?

ELVIRA.

     And a back-up, on floppy.

(He looks at it.)

     I know that you can't love me. I understand.

     Just take me in your arms and get me off your hands.

DON.

     I have no retort. My brain is weak.

ELVIRA.

     Well. The ball is in your court.

DON and ELVIRA.

     So to speak.

ELVIRA.

     I guess you also cut some deal.

DON.

     Si, Si.

ELVIRA.

     For eternal sex, no doubt. You heel.

DON.

     Not exactly.

ELVIRA.

     But I don't accuse you. It's fine.

     You're the creature that lusts.

     I'm the being that will always pine.

DON.

     Elvira, I'm sorry.

ELVIRA.

     I'm not here to play *memento mori.*

     I found out the hard way

     That you can't make someone want you.

     The best I can do

     Is love you, and haunt you,

     Again and again and again.

     Madrid, 1600. Moscow, 1610.

DON.

     Paris. The Hotel de Ville.

ELVIRA.
> The ferris wheel in Vienna.

DON.
> The castle in Castile.

ELVIRA.
> I almost nailed you in Dien Bien Phu.

DON.
> Ah, right. The Hotel Déjà Vû.
> Champagne in Kinshasa.

ELVIRA.
> A bubbly time.

DON.
> Beneath a lime tree in Lhasa.

ELVIRA.
> Sub ... lime.

DON.
> Remember the shellfish? The garden maze?

ELVIRA.
> Yes, yes. The good old days ...

DON.
> Elvira, I can't love you only to lose you.

ELVIRA.
> You are so *selfish!*

DON.
> I can't send you to hell for eternal torment.

ELVIRA.
> Hell doesn't terrify me.
> I've been in hell for centuries.
> The hell of not having you, Don Juan.
> Not having you — or anyone.
> The only way I'll ever rest
> Is to lie in your arms again.
> So my beloved enemy, hated friend,
> Won't you love me and kill me?
> That's my humble petition. Amen.

(Pause.)
> Help me, partner.

DON.

I can't. But there's a good reason.

ELVIRA.

Have you no decency? Have you no heart, sir?

DON.

No. Listen —

ELVIRA.

I don't give a fart, sir, for your excuses.

What are they to me, victim of your abuses?

DON.

Elvira, please.

ELVIRA.

We have a bond, Juan!

All right. This visit didn't work, alack.

But don't you worry — jerk. I'll be back!

(She exits. The clock strikes eight. Leporello enters from right.)

LEPORELLO.   So I guess we're immortal for another day. Want a Dorito?

DON.   It was Elvira.

LEPORELLO.   *Aaaaaaaah! (The Doritos go flying. Crossing himself.)* Help me, God, help me, help me.

DON.   Not only that. She can't die until I make love to her again.

LEPORELLO.   Wowzer. Hard cheese on Vera, huh. Okay. I'll pack tonight, we'll call the movers in the morning. But shit, look what time it is! You gotta get on your stick. *(Starts out, comes back.)* What's the matter? Something wrong?

DON.   She offered me the chance of doing something noble — and I turned her down.

LEPORELLO.   Well sure you turned her down! I mean — *POOF.* Remember? What could you do?

DON.   I could've slept with her.

LEPORELLO.   Excuse me? I couldn't hear you, you had your head up your ass.

DON.   Maybe I'll read for a while.

LEPORELLO.   Did you say "read"?

DON.   Some Keats, for example.

LEPORELLO. Hello? D.J.?

DON. I'm reading, Leporello.

LEPORELLO. Very edifying. However, you gotta vote for sexual congress by midnight or we hit our term limits.

DON. *(Reading.)*

"... many a time
I have been half in love with easeful death ..."

LEPORELLO. *(To audience.)* Can somebody help me out here? Any of you ladies feel like a tumble? Here's your big chance. Sleep with the Don, tell all your friends. Spend a night with a living legend, only do it by midnight. *(To a woman in the audience.)* How about you? You look like a nice person and you would have my literally undying gratitude. Donny, I have a woman here in the audience, first woman here on the end? Rather mature, but she is gorgeous!

DON. I've slept with her.

LEPORELLO. Will you copulate, please?

DON. I didn't know you were that attached to this world.

LEPORELLO. I *love* this world.

DON. *(Throwing down his book.)* Well *I don't love this fucking world!*

LEPORELLO. You just gotta give it a better chance, Don.

DON. Better than four hundred years?

LEPORELLO. You always wanted to be a household name, and you *are* one! You're in the dictionary!

DON. Yes. Don Juan. The biggest dick in history. Famous for fucking.

LEPORELLO. People envy you!

DON. Pigeons fuck. Pigs fuck. Goldfish fuck. Who envies them?

LEPORELLO. *I* do, frankly. Given my social calendar.

DON. Leporello, we've seen twenty generations pass from the earth. Aren't you tired of seeing people die?

LEPORELLO. Me? *Hell* no.

DON. Sleep with another woman? Why should I?

LEPORELLO. Why? I'll tell you why. Because *you owe me,* pal. That's right. You *owe* me. I have never once said this in

400 years, but you got an obligation. You took my life away. You give it back to me. You don't like the bargain you made? That's too bad. You want to go to hell? Fine. That's your business. But you got no fucking right to take me along with you. You had no fucking right in the first place. I am an innocent bystander here. I was an honest man! So either you leverage me outa this deal, or you find somebody to sleep with and keep us alive one more day. I'm sorry to put this so bluntly.

DON. No. No. You have every right. *I'm* sorry. *(A silence.)*

LEPORELLO. Hey. Hey. What about this kid? Your daughter? *(A knock at the door.)* Live, Don, and you'll get to meet her.

DON. That child is lost.

LEPORELLO. She has to be *some*place. We'll go find her! *(Another knock at the door.)* What do you say, we'll go hunt up Wendy-Sandy-Wendy and you can have a family reunion.

DON. What would I do if I found my daughter? What could I say to her if she came knocking at that door? *(Knock at the door.)*

LEPORELLO. You say clean up your room, like all fathers. I look forward to meeting this tike! I'll be godfather!

DON. Even living forever I can't believe I'll ever get to see her.

LEPORELLO. Yeah, but this is your daughter— *(Just then, he opens the door to Mike and Zoey, 23.)*

ZOEY. Hello.

LEPORELLO. Well isn't this delightful. Donny — behold. A fair young maiden on our doorstep!

MIKE. Hi, Don.

DON.
> "Who are these coming to the sacrifice?
> To what green altar, O mysterious priest,
> Leadst thou that heifer lowing at the skies?"

MIKE. Uh, Lefty. This is my girlfriend, Zoey.

LEPORELLO. Donny, this is Mike's girlfriend Zoey.

ZOEY.
> "Fair youth beneath the trees,
> Thou canst not leave thy song,
> Nor ever can those trees be bare."

76

DON.

"Bold lover, never, never canst thou kiss,
Though winning near the goal."

ZOEY.

"Yet do not grieve.
She cannot fade though thou hast not thy bliss."

DON.

"Forever wilt thou love — "

ZOEY.

" — and she be fair."

— John Keats.

(An angelic chorus is heard, for a moment.) Hello.

DON.   Hello.

ZOEY.   I'm really sorry, us just coming in like this.

DON.   No. Please. Come in further.

ZOEY.   *(Holds out a piece of candy.)* Happy Halloween.

DON.   I'm sorry, your name is...?

ZOEY.   Zoey. I live in 9B, down the hall — ?

DON.   Don Johnson. How do you do. *(He kisses her hand and the angelic chorus is heard again, briefly.)*

ZOEY.   And this is Mike.

MIKE.   Nine-A...?

DON.   *(Not looking at Mike, eyes on Zoey.)* Yes, I know Mike ...

ZOEY.   Can I have my hand back now?

DON.   *(Releasing her hand.)* I'm sorry.

LEPORELLO.   But come on, kids, sit down! We were just partying here! And look, Don, they brought us a present! *(He starts to take a gift-wrapped box from Zoey.)*

ZOEY.   Actually that's a gift for Mike. It's a tie.

DON.   So you know Keats.

ZOEY.   Oh I don't really know about Keats. I don't really know anything about anything. It's just I learned that poem in high school and those words are so beautiful. I think if I lived to be five hundred years old I couldn't come up with something as beautiful as that.

DON.   Yes, Johnny wrote some wonderful things.

ZOEY.   He's dead now, you know.

DON.   Yet somehow I feel as if I knew him.

LEPORELLO.   Donny *is* 400 years old. *(Aside to Don.)* Is this girl something, Dondi?

DON.   Suddenly — I don't know why — I have a strange soup of emotions boiling around my heart.

LEPORELLO.   So *consummate! Consummate!* You move in, I'll distract the lunk. — *(To Zoey and Mike.)* Well, my newfound friends. What brings you to our humble commode?

ZOEY.   Actually, we came over to ask if we should sleep together. *(Small pause.)*

DON and LEPORELLO.   Excuse me?

MIKE.   Zoey, you shouldn't'a put it like that.

ZOEY.   That *is* our question, isn't it? Mr. Johnson — should Mike and me sleep together?

LEPORELLO.   Or you and God-knows-who-else-in-this-wide-world, right? *Liqueur?*

DON.   Why are you asking *me* this?

MIKE.   Well we figured you'd know something on the subject.

ZOEY.   Since every time we see you you're either walking into the building with a woman, or you're letting some woman out of the building ... Mike said maybe you're running a house of prostitution. Am I right, Mike?

MIKE.   You're right, Zo.

ZOEY.   *I* said you're just a real Don Juan.

MIKE.   Zoey, come on.

DON.   A pale imitation, actually. *(The door opens and Sandy appears.)*

SANDY.   That man is a *vampire!* He sucks the blood of women and then he throws their lifeless bodies away! And don't say I didn't warn you! *(Leporello closes the door.)*

LEPORELLO.   Political candidate.

DON.   You were saying — ?

MIKE.   Yeah. Zoey and me've been going out for a while now.

ZOEY.   Seven years tomorrow.

MIKE.   All Saints' Day.

DON.   That's a while.

ZOEY.   And me and Mike pledged eternal love on like our second date.

MIKE.   But we've never slept together.

ZOEY.   We've never slept with anybody.

MIKE.   Except ourselves.

ZOEY.   Separately, we mean.

LEPORELLO.   If you don't mind my asking, how did you two manage to avoid having sex for seven short years?

MIKE.   I don't know. It never came up.

ZOEY.   There are so many things to do. We take walks.

MIKE.   And we talk.

ZOEY.   About — you know — the meaning of life.

MIKE.   Ontology. The categorical imperative.

ZOEY.   Stuff like that. And we spend a lot of time agreeing about things. It's like, I'll say I like something and Mike'll say *he* likes it, or he'll say *he* likes something and I'll say *I* like it. *(Holding up the skull.)* What an interesting vase.

MIKE.   Wow. Very interesting.

ZOEY.   Anyway, these days it's like everybody's slept with somebody besides themselves.

MIKE.   Down at the health club there's guys who've slept with two and three women already.

DON.   No.

MIKE.   Yeah.

ZOEY.   And *I* said, there's that man down the hall. Don Johnson.

MIKE.   "Who *is* that guy anyway?"

ZOEY.   I say that all the time. Am I right, Mike?

MIKE.   You're right, Zo.

ZOEY.   So what do you think? Sex? Or no sex?

LEPORELLO.   But listen, Mike. I got a very rare stereopticon I wanted to show you.

MIKE.   Oh yeah?

LEPORELLO.   Right this way. *(Leading Mike out R., to Don and Zoey.)* We'll leave you two alone for a moment. *(Leporello exits with Mike.)*

ZOEY.   I've never met a butler before. It's not exactly what I expected.

DON.   Lefty's not entirely typical of the breed. *(He moves toward her, she moves toward the abstrolabe.)*

ZOEY.   Where did you get this lamp?

DON.   It's an astrolabe, actually. Antiquated instrument for charting the stars. You can see the stars better if the lights are low. I hope you don't mind.

ZOEY.   No, that's so much nicer. *(She turns off the lamp.)*

DON.

And here's a happy bit of happenstance.
Like a metaphor of your quandary,
An album titled "Shall We Dance?"

(He puts on music.)

ZOEY.   I love to dance.

DON.   Do you really? *(They dance.)*

ZOEY.   It's funny. I don't even know you and I trust you. Like a father, or something. *(Mike looks in from Leporello's room.)*

MIKE.   How are you doing, Zo?

ZOEY.   Fine. We're dancing.

MIKE.   Oh. Okay ... *(Mike goes back out.)*

ZOEY.   So what about sex, Mr. Johnson?

DON.   Yes, what about sex ... *(Mike appears again in the doorway.)*

MIKE.   You ought to see this, Zoey. It's great.

ZOEY.   Maybe later on, Mike.

MIKE.   Okay ... *(Mike goes back out.)*

ZOEY.   So tell me about sex. Is it really wonderful? Is it blissful kissfuls of rapturous night in an everlasting garden of earthly delight?

DON.   How did you get that idea?

ZOEY.   I read it on a bus. Or, will Mike and me go bad if we sleep together?

DON.   It's just biology, isn't it?

ZOEY.   It's true.

DON.   And one only has so much time. *(Checks his watch.)* Venice is sinking and the polar caps are melting. Tomorrow we die. If not sooner.

ZOEY.   That's true. But will Mike and me still be happy? Or will we be happier than ever?

DON.   Far happier.

ZOEY.   You've slept with lots of people. Are *you* happy?

DON.   Terribly.

ZOEY.   You don't look very happy.

DON.   I don't...?

ZOEY.   No, I look at you and somehow I feel terribly sad.

DON.   Maybe I'm not the right person to judge by.

ZOEY.   It's just like this opera we saw called *Don Giovanni*. Have you ever heard of this opera *Don Giovanni*?

DON.   I think so.

ZOEY.   Actually it's Don Juan in another language, by — what was his name? — Moss Hart.

DON.   Moss Hart.

ZOEY.   Do you know the Don Juan story?

DON.   Ah, vaguely.

ZOEY.   Don Juan sleeps with all these women but he still doesn't live happily forever after. Hell opens up and he falls into the fiery pit to be punished for all eternity.

DON.   It is only a fable.

ZOEY.   No, no, it's real. Because Don Juan doesn't sleep with all those women with love in his heart. If you live without love, you've given up your soul. Am I right, Don?

DON.   You're right, Zoey.

ZOEY.   It's like my mother. She slept with somebody for one night and had me. I never knew my mother or my father but it's like God spoke to them personally. It's like he said, you did this for pleasure, but now I'll show you the important part. Here. Remember this? *(As if holding out a baby.)* It's love.

DON.   So you're an orphan ...

ZOEY.   Yes. But I do hope to meet my parents somehow in this lifetime. Whoever they are. Now you look sadder than ever.

DON.   I'm simply overwhelmed by the ways of the Almighty, that the universe could create a creature like you and bring you to my door tonight of all nights.

ZOEY.   I'm sort of overwhelmed by the Almighty every day.

DON.   I'm sure it's mutual.

ZOEY.   You know, Mike and me were going out for some supper right now. Would you like to come along?

DON.   I'd love to. *(Leporello enters.)*

LEPORELLO.   So how is it going in here?

DON.   Zoey just invited me to dinner.

LEPORELLO.   Indeed, indeed? *(Aside to Don.)* All is well, Tristan?

MIKE.   Zoey ...

ZOEY.   What's the matter, Mike?

MIKE.   It's our anniversary. I thought we were gonna go out by ourselves.

ZOEY.   But Don is helping us out. Isn't that right, Mike?

MIKE.   Yeah, but ...

ZOEY.   So where should we go?

DON.   I know a fantastic place. I haven't been there since 1867 — 1967 — 1987.

LEPORELLO.   And how are you going to pay for this, Mr. Rockefeller?

DON.   I can pawn the astrolabe on the way. We'll be eating the stars off of our plates. We'll pick the tails of comets out of our teeth and set the pits of planets on the rims of our saucers.

ZOEY.   No. It's our treat. For helping us out. Right, Mike?

MIKE.   Well ...

DON.   Excellent. I'll meet you downstairs.

ZOEY.   I guess I'd better go change.

DON.   You don't have to change a thing.

ZOEY.   I could change anyway. *(Don kisses her hand.)*

DON.   *A bientôt.*

ZOEY.   *A bientôt* too. *(Mike and Zoey start out. As they head out the door.)*

MIKE.   I thought you were going to go like that.

ZOEY.   But we have a guest with us, Mike ... *(They exit.)*

LEPORELLO.   So? Well? Is this perfect? Is it great? How'd you do?

DON.   I didn't do anything.

LEPORELLO.   I know. You're gonna do it in the cloak room at the restaurant. I *love* that.

DON.   I'm not going to do anything.

LEPORELLO.   Wait wait wait wait wait wait wait wait.

DON.   Anywhere.

LEPORELLO.   Donald, you are murdering us. Will you seduce this girl, please?

DON.   That is not a girl.

LEPORELLO.   It's a girl! What, you can't recognize one anymore? She's a girl. She has girlitude.

DON.   No, that is a living, breathing radiance.

LEPORELLO.   So up the wattage!

DON.   And corrupt her?

LEPORELLO.   You can't corrupt anybody anymore! Everybody's corrupt now! *(Todd appears at the door.)*

TODD.   I am going to murder you, Johnson.

DON.   You can't. Goodbye, Todd. *(Shuts the door.)*

LEPORELLO.   You like this girl, am I right, Don?

DON.   She's poetry. I will not sleep with her.

LEPORELLO.   Okay. You don't want to do it with her, then you better find some other woman and you can scan this poetry into infinity. Please, Don. I got everything to live for.

DON.   Oh yes, like what?

LEPORELLO.   Like my youth! I'm still young! No, I'm not, I'm 450 years old. Like my wonderful job! What'm I talking about, I'm a fucking slave. Like my living conditions! Like...! Like...! Okay, so I have no reason to live. Does that mean I have no reason to live? Give me a coupla weeks to work out this paradox. Give me the chance to see the bluebells again. Give me the chance to find out what a bluebell *is.* I swear. I'll never ask for new underwear again. *(Knock at door.)*

MEPHISTOPHELES.   *(From off.)* 'Allo? Anybody there? Exterminator!

LEPORELLO.   The hell is this? Bug sprayers? At this time of night? *(Don opens the door and Mephistopheles enters — in drag. He wear a gray dress/uniform with enormous breasts, a blonde Mae West wig, and a tank of pesticide with a hose. He uses a French accent.)*

MEPHISTOPHELES.

        Bon soir, messieurs! Acme Pest Control.

        Is there something I can kill in your chateau?

        I have the poison and the expertise.

(Aside, to audience.)

        Actually, it's me again. Mephistopheles.

LEPORELLO.

>*Mademoiselle,* please — *avanti!*
>
>We were just sitting around and, uh, reading some
>>Dante.
>
>*Figure-toi,* Don *alde,* what a *belle* surpreez.

(Mephistopheles coughs.)

DON.

>Are you all right, Miss?

MEPHISTOPHELES.

>Just a leetle *(Cough.)* wheeze.

DON.

>Are you sure there isn't some mistake?

MEPHISTOPHELES.

>*Mais non!* You have roaches? Vermin? *Snakes?*

LEPORELLO.

>Donny, an opportune *au pair!*
>
>Opportune if you ignore the facial hair.
>
>All you gotta do is bed this hag.

(To us.)

>Jesus. Looks like Dick Nixon in drag.

(To Don.)

>Move in, champ. Start to flirt.

MEPHISTOPHELES.

>*Alors, messieurs.* You want a squirt?

(Squirts out of his pesticide hose.)

DON.

>I'm sorry, Miss, but it's getting late
>
>And I have an important dinner date.

*(There's a loud crack of thunder, and Mephistopheles tears off his
wig, revealing himself. Demonic chorus.)*

MEPHISTOPHELES.

>You have a date with *me,* Don Juan!
>
>At midnight, in my deepest dungeon!
>
>I'll spit you in the hottest hole in Hades,
>
>And you'll roast right where you like it —
>
>There among the ladies.
>
>For a billion billion eons
>
>You'll glow like truth's own torch.

Obey the contract, peons — or scorch!

DON.

I'll see you at twelve.

MEPHISTOPHELES.

Yes, when I come to carry you to hell!

(Don goes out. To Leporello.)

Boo.

(Leporello faints and falls to the floor.)

Lights!

END OF ACT TWO

ACT THREE

Eternity

The clock strikes nine as lights come up on Mephistopheles in his old get-up. Leporello lies on the floor where he fainted.

MEPHISTOPHELES.
    Forgive me, mortals! The devil made me do it!
    I had no choice! I I I I — oh, screw it.
    Must I, the Very Nearly All Powerful,
    Explain my acts to every begging little get?
    The Don was reneging,
    I was calling in the debt.
    As for the moral of the scene,
    If you'll trust a devil tubercular:
    What goes around ... is circular.
    And behold the circulating creature.
(He indicates Leporello.)
    This lump of gristle here.
    Were I to whistle, this manic man
    Would instinctively bristle up in panic fear
    Of losing his hundred fifty pounds of flesh.
    Seventy inches of nerve end — serving what end,
    Swerving from lust to anxiety and back again?
    And yet, dismantle the temple of history,
    Scan the universe through and through,
    This humble slob is nature's greatest mystery.
(Leporello snores.)
    I can't explain it. Can *you?*
    But hark —
(The window opens.)
    — a visitor.
(Todd comes in the window with a gun.)
    Todd with a pistol. Heaven forfend.
    I am invisible. Attend.

(Mephistopheles continues to observe, invisible.)
TODD.   Get up.
LEPORELLO.   *(Starts up in fright.)* Huh — ?
MEPHISTOPHELES.   Panic fear.
LEPORELLO.   Oh. It's you.
TODD.   I said get up. On your feet, Jackson.
LEPORELLO.   Sorry. I think you got the wrong guy.
TODD.   I said *up,* Jackson! *Los!*
LEPORELLO.   *(To us.)* Do I resemble the Don, or have I entered fairyland? *(He gets up.)*
TODD.   See this? Do you see what I have here?
LEPORELLO.   *(Unfazed, knowing it can't hurt him.)* Oh my goodness. Is that a pistol. No, please, please, I beg you, don't shoot me. Mercy. Mercy.
TODD.   I'm going to kill you, Jackson.
LEPORELLO.   I wish you could, *mon ami.*
MEPHISTOPHELES.   Would he say the same to *me?*
TODD.   I'm going to do it nice and slowly.
LEPORELLO.   You mind if I pour myself a drink?
TODD.   Yes I do.
LEPORELLO.   *(Moving past him.)* 'Scuse me. — You know what your problem is, Todd?
TODD.   I'm an asshole.
LEPORELLO.   You're an asshole. So you know this?
TODD.   Self-knowledge. It's the beginning of wisdom.
LEPORELLO.   Great. May I suggest a rectum-ectomy? Scram.
TODD.   This is where the asshole redeems himself. With hot lead.
LEPORELLO.   You little tease.
TODD.   Bastard! My life was totally meaningless till I met Wendy.
LEPORELLO.   Sandy.
TODD.   Sandy. After I met her my life was still meaningless, but at least I found somebody who'd take my shit. These have been the five best weeks of my life! Why did you do it? Why did you take her away from me?
LEPORELLO.   Okay. I confess. It's a medical problem. See, if I don't sleep with a different woman every day I get these

terrible headaches.

TODD. Really.

LEPORELLO. JFK told me he had the same thing. They call it the spermatic migraine.

TODD. I get those.

LEPORELLO. Also, women find me irresistibly attractive. Do *you* find me attractive, Todd?

TODD. Well ...

LEPORELLO. Never mind. Then I go out tonight to find a woman and — *boom* — I meet this woman.

TODD. Sandy.

LEPORELLO. Sandy. And I realized, this woman is luminous. She's intoxicating. She's sublime! She's fucked *up*. But she's sublime. And we fell in love.

TODD. Swine. Look your last, Jackson. You die and I get Sandy back.

LEPORELLO. Lucky gal, huh. Are these your glasses?

TODD. *(Puts on his glasses.)* Who are you?

LEPORELLO. Who am *I*, sir? Who are *you*? Who is anybody? You ask me a metaphysical question when I have a whiskey in my hand? Begone! *(Todd shoots at him. The chamber clicks, empty.)*

TODD. I'm going to get some bullets. *(He exits through the window.)*

LEPORELLO. *(To us.)* I'm going to hell. Fine. But if I have to spend eternity with that asshole, I am gonna make some noise. Nine thirty-five. Maybe a Haagen-Dazs bar ... *(Leporello starts out right, but Sandy appears from there with the knife.)*

SANDY. Hold it right there.

LEPORELLO. Sandy...!

SANDY. Thank you for remembering my name. You pimp.

LEPORELLO. Y'know, Don would love to talk to you.

SANDY. Yes and I'd like to talk to *him*.

LEPORELLO. He just went out.

SANDY. Good. Your lifeless body will be here to greet him.

LEPORELLO. Actually, my lifeless body has a couple of hours yet.

SANDY. Be my guest and dial yourself a hearse. Die! Die! Die! Die! Die! *(She stabs him repeatedly, to no effect.)*

LEPORELLO. Sandy.

SANDY. Die, die, die, die, die ... *(Still no effect.)* You're not dead.

LEPORELLO. Uh, no.

SANDY. Why, why, why, why? This is a Toledo blade!

LEPORELLO. Ironically, so am I. But as they say at Ohio State: Toledo, too late.

SANDY. Why are you still standing here?

LEPORELLO. Well. You can't kill me.

SANDY. Uh-huh.

LEPORELLO. Or the Don.

SANDY. Uh-huh.

LEPORELLO. Not till midnight. Unless the Don sleeps with somebody. Never mind. It's complicated.

SANDY. Yeah. My life story. I try murder in the first and the victim's invincible.

LEPORELLO. Sorry.

SANDY. So I can't win. Even before I've started I'm beat.

LEPORELLO. Want to join me?

SANDY. What is it?

LEPORELLO. Bourbon on the rocks?

SANDY. No, just neat. — You know why I do this?

LEPORELLO. Lemme guess. Your mother? A second cousin? A traumatic afternoon with your Aunt Bee?

SANDY. No, it's me. Me, me, me, me, me.

LEPORELLO. Hey. You think you're a mess? Ziggy Freud tried to analyze me and he gave up. He sent me to an exorcist.

SANDY. Sigmund Freud died in 1939.

LEPORELLO. I know. I was a pallbearer. Very sad day. *(Holding out her drink.)* Well — Sandra. Or is it Alexandra?

SANDY. Actually, it's Allison.

LEPORELLO. Allison...? *(An angelic chorus is heard.)* Did you say *Allison...?!*

SANDY. Allison Goody.

MEPHISTOPHELES.

    My word, I think he's getting a woody.

LEPORELLO.

> Allison — could I ask something strange,
> Put the horse behind the cart?
> Would you take your hand and feel my heart?
> Is it...?

SANDY.

> It's beating, but *fast*. Oh boy!

LEPORELLO.

> Beating? It's Beethoven!
> It's the fuckin' Ode to Joy!

SANDY.

> The fibrillation is intense!

LEPORELLO.

> So's the genital stimulation.
> No offense.
> What are you, the Queen of Araby?

SANDY.

> What're *you*? The answer to my therapy?

LEPORELLO.

> Oh God, I *am* in fairyland!

SANDY.

> And invulnerable, too...? What ... stamina.

MEPHISTOPHELES.

> Fascinating.

SANDY.

> My animus.

LEPORELLO.

> My anima.
> Y'know, Channel 37 is screening film noir.

SANDY.

> We could watch it on the couch,
> Or in your boudoir.

LEPORELLO.

> The sheets are pretty scary.
> Would you tell me to shove it?

SANDY.

> On the contrary. I *love* it.

(Sandy and Leporello exit to his bedroom. The clock strikes ten.)

MEPHISTOPHELES.

But I sense another visitor getting nearer.

Some Halloween seeker after treats or tricks?

(Elvira enters.)

No. The fair Elvira.

They really *must* get that door fixed.

(Elvira looks about the room, Mephistopheles following close behind her.)

Buenas tardes.

(Elvira turns, startled.)

ELVIRA.

You, Iniquitous...?

MEPHISTOPHELES.

Me. The Ubiquitous.

ELVIRA.

Long time no see.

Say, seven thousand score days.

MEPHISTOPHELES.

Is it that long now? I am amazed.

No hard feelings about our little arrangement,

I hope.

ELVIRA.

Why should there be?

You were just the hangman. I supplied the rope.

I myself erased the narrow line

Between cupidity and stupidity.

MEPHISTOPHELES.

You just missed your beau.

ELVIRA.

Don Juan...?

MEPHISTOPHELES.

The lad's gone out with ...

ELVIRA.

A lass. I know.

I saw him leave, he and his young friend.

MEPHISTOPHELES.

Then you come here — to what end?

To dope an apple with poison?

A fruitless cabal.
To spike his wine with Spanish fly
Bootlessly hoping he'll bed you after all?

ELVIRA.

Oh God, oh God, if I could only vanish, die
Before I go mad.
I am going mad, you know.

MEPHISTOPHELES.

Why, Elvira? Why are you here?

ELVIRA.

Because tomorrow he'll disappear,
And all these things will be gone.
Knowing now I'm after him he'll depart at dawn.
Another twenty years, maybe I'll find him again
And again he'll evade me.
I come, he leaves.

MEPHISTOPHELES.

Fond lady ...

ELVIRA.   *(Through tears.)*

But really. I don't grieve.

MEPHISTOPHELES.

My dear, I shouldn't do this, but ...

ELVIRA.

Something tells me I'm going to rue this.
(Mephistopheles produces a contract.)
What. What's that?

MEPHISTOPHELES.

A contract.

ELVIRA.

Is it — ?

MEPHISTOPHELES.

The Don's. I won't dissemble.

ELVIRA.

Why do I suddenly tremble...?

MEPHISTOPHELES.

I give you a choice, *cherie.*
You can read this and stop all wondering,
Or I can blind the Don

And he'll sleep with you by blundering.
Knowledge or rest, which will it be?

ELVIRA.

There's no contest. This.

(She reaches for it. He pulls it away.)

MEPHISTOPHELES.

You lose me. This? Why?

ELVIRA.

Because he has to choose me.
It can't be just a lie.

MEPHISTOPHELES.

Fascinating. Well, then, scope this.

(Elvira takes the contract and reads.)

Though you may wish you'd made the other trade.

ELVIRA.   *(Reading.)*

Oh no. No ...

MEPHISTOPHELES.

Yes. It's hopeless, I'm afraid.
You and the Don have been farcing in and out of doors
Because his contract is the opposite of yours.

ELVIRA.

It can't be true.

MEPHISTOPHELES.

It is, of course.

ELVIRA.

What a fool. What a fool ...

MEPHISTOPHELES.

Do you hate him all the more,
Now you've read this?

ELVIRA.

I love him all the more, of course. Poor man.

MEPHISTOPHELES.

I simply don't comprehend this.
He might have told you.

ELVIRA.

He wanted to save me from despair.
Why did *you* tell, Satan?

(Pause.)

MEPHISTOPHELES.

    I don't honestly know …

ELVIRA.

    So I can never sleep with the Don.

    I'm done for. All hope is gone.

MEPHISTOPHELES.

    Give up, Elvira. That's what's best.

    What you seek's a mere …

ELVIRA.

    Chimera.

MEPHISTOPHELES.

    Rest. Rest.

(Don enters with Zoey and Mike. Mephistopheles and Elvira draw back and listen.)

ZOEY.   How do you know all this stuff? Poetry and cities and restaurants…. It's like you've been everywhere and done everything.

DON.   Well I *am* four hundred years old.

ZOEY.   You know I halfway believe it?

DON.   Maybe we should open some champagne and celebrate your anniversary. What do you say, Mike? *(Mike says nothing.)*

ZOEY.   Some days I really wish I could make a deal with the devil.

MEPHISTOPHELES.   Oh…?

DON.   Deal with the devil?

ZOEY.   No, really. See, I've really had a pretty happy life in general only I don't know anything about anything. You seem pretty miserable but you sure do know about things. So sometimes I think I'd give up some of this happiness for something a little more exciting in the rest of my life.

DON.   You can't mean that.

ZOEY.   I'd be glad to be sad, if the circumstances were right … *(She sees Elvira just then, and lets out a shriek. Elvira simply walks out without a word, dropping her fan as she goes.)* Who was that? Was that a friend of yours? Was it somebody you've slept with? *(Don says nothing.)* Don?

DON.   Would you excuse me? *(He picks up the fan and goes*

PROPERTY OF
HIGH POINT PUBLIC LIBRARY
HIGH POINT, NORTH CAROLINA

out.) Elvira...?!

ZOEY. What an evening, huh.

MIKE. Yeah, listen. You want to come back to my place and talk for a while?

ZOEY. I never did give you your present.

MIKE. So come back to my place and you can give it to me there.

ZOEY. Right here is fine. Happy anniversary. *(Mike takes the box from her.)* Go ahead. Open it. I mean, you know it's a tie.

MIKE. Who are you?

ZOEY. What...?

MIKE. Who are you? Who am I talking to, here?

ZOEY. What do you mean?

MIKE. I mean who am I talking to? Were you always like this and I never noticed, or is this new, tonight?

ZOEY. Like what? I don't know what you ...

MIKE. Like a guy recites poetry and kisses your hand and suddenly you're a different person — ? Who are you now? Are you the person who didn't hear me talking at the dinner table? Or are you the person who swore eternal love with me seven years ago tomorrow?

ZOEY. Well I can't be that person exactly, I mean it was seven years ago ...

MIKE. Yeah and I guess I'm not enough for you now, you have to make a deal with the devil to be happy, is that it?

ZOEY. No, I ...

MIKE. You want something more exciting in your life than just being happy.

ZOEY. No ...

MIKE. Hang out with somebody who don't agree with you all the time, somebody like Don, maybe.

ZOEY. Don't say these things, Mike.

MIKE. You don't want to sleep with me, maybe sleep with him instead, huh.

ZOEY. I don't want to sleep with him. How can you say that?

MIKE. What does this say, right here? *(Reads off the paper tag on her gift.)* "With love from Zoey." Love. Zoey. How did this word get here? Were you lying when you wrote this word?

ZOEY.   No.

MIKE.   "Love" — ? Eternal love, remember?

ZOEY.   I do love you. But ...

MIKE.   But what?

ZOEY.   What if we're not so eternal after all?

MIKE.   Two strangers can learn how to love each other. How can two people who love each other turn into strangers?

ZOEY.   We're not strangers.

MIKE.   Yeah. We're strangers now. The minute people start using the word strangers, they're strangers.

ZOEY.   I don't know, Mike. I don't know what's going on with me tonight. I feel so sorry. I just feel so ... really sorry and I don't even know why.

MIKE.   Well. Happy anniversary. Happy Halloween. Happy everything. 'Bye, Zo. (*He crumples up the paper tag and exits. Mephistopheles picks up the crumpled paper.*)

MEPHISTOPHELES.

Answer me, mortals.

Time scrolls an animal from dust

And in the breast of that same creature

Sets a heart that glows

Like a delicate, pencil-thin taper.

Why do you blow out that flame?

Why would you crumple that heart, like paper?

(*Don enters.*)

ZOEY.   Did you find your friend?

DON.   No.... Where's Mike?

ZOEY.   Oh. He's gone.

DON.   What's the matter?

ZOEY.   (*Backing off.*) I think you better stay away from me.

DON.   What is it?

ZOEY.   I think you're the devil. Mike said I was acting like ...

DON.   Like what?

ZOEY.   But what does it really matter if two people sleep together.

DON.   Sleep together.

ZOEY.   Yeah, I mean it's just biology, right? Venice is melting and the ice caps are sinking.

DON.   What are you talking about.

ZOEY.   *About the two of us sleeping together.* You and me. How can this happen? What have you done to me?

DON.   Zoey, I swear.

ZOEY.   I think I just broke his heart. How could I do that? This morning I had everything. I was so happy. Somehow I gave it all away ...

DON.   Go back to him. Go on.

ZOEY.   I don't think I can. *(Leporello enters.)*

LEPORELLO.   Don. Don. Listen. Remember I didn't have a reason to live? Boy do I have a reason to live, and she's right in that room.

DON.   I can't talk right now, Leporello.

LEPORELLO.   You got any condoms I could borrow? I mean, you know, have?

DON.   Listen to me.

LEPORELLO.   So did you get lucky? Are we going to live?

DON.   No we're not.

LEPORELLO.   Donny, Donny, you gotta keep me alive. I haven't been this blissful since Marie Antoinette's scrub lady.

DON.   I'm sorry, Leporello. We're dying tonight.

LEPORELLO.   No we are *not* dying tonight. You gotta do somebody and do it fast, and right now you only got one prospect. *(Zoey is moving toward them.)* And she's coming right this way. *(Todd enters with the gun.)*

TODD.   Dick Jackson?

DON.   Don Johnson.

TODD.   Here's where you die. Say your prayers. *(He levels the gun at Don.)*

ZOEY.   Oh my God...!

DON.   Zoey, stand behind me.

TODD.   When you get to hell, tell them Todd the Rat sent you. *(He fires the pistol, but Don keeps standing.)* You bastard! You bastard! You ruined my life! *(He fires again.)* You should be dead ... *(He fires again.)* YOU SHOULD BE DEAD! *(Todd runs out.)*

DON.   Zoey...?

ZOEY. Don...? *(Mike enters.)*

MIKE. Zoey ...

ZOEY. Mike!

LEPORELLO. *(Warning.)* Don ...

ZOEY. Don ...

MIKE. *(Threatening.)* Don ...

DON. Zoey — are you all right?

ZOEY. There's no bullet holes! There's no blood or anything!

DON. I guess he must've missed.

ZOEY. How could he miss? He fired right at you! You could be standing here dead right now! *(Backing away from him toward Mike.)* What are you...? Are you really a vampire?

DON. Yes I am. But the man standing behind you isn't. He's flesh and blood, and he loves you. Don't you, Mike?

MIKE. Well sure, I mean ...

LEPORELLO. *(Pulling Don aside.)* Don.

DON. Lefty.

LEPORELLO. Let's keep our priorities straight here. A), we gotta stay alive. B), it's — *(The clock strikes eleven, very fast.)* — eleven o'clock. C), everything else. Now I still see a glimmer of hope here with young Zo-Zo. Sure, there's complications, but you got an hour till the clock says bong. And don't forget — you are the *Dong.*

DON. No, Leporello. *(Sandy enters.)*

SANDY. What the hell is going on out here?

LEPORELLO. Sweetheart, you got any horny acquaintances might want to come over for a quick and stormy relationship?

SANDY. Oh *that's* nice. That's very cute.

LEPORELLO. No no no no no. Not for me. For him!

SANDY. Goodbye! *(She turns to leave, as Elvira appears at the door, dressed as she had been in Act One.)*

ELVIRA.

     Don Juan.

DON.

     Dona Elvira.

(Elvira speaks without hearing Don Juan till noted.)

ELVIRA.

For the last time I come to your door.
But worry not, señor.

DON.

Worry? What for?

ELVIRA.

I've not come back to ask my wonted favor.

DON.

Ask me and it's yours forever.

ELVIRA.

I've come to say farewell
Before I join the convent of our saviour.

DON.

Elvira, please, not another rhyme!

ELVIRA.

I'm going to spend my days amending my soul,
Atoning for my crimes.

DON.

Will you listen to me?

ELVIRA.

I myself built the cage I'm in.

DON.

Darling, darling —

ELVIRA.

Utter misery.

DON.

Will you be quiet, darling?

ELVIRA.

That's the wages of sin.

(Stops.)

Did you say "darling"?

DON.   Zoey, the answer to your question of the night is: yes
you should. Yes. Sleep together. Because to lie in the arms of
another person is one of the greatest and most glorious things
one can do on this emerald earth — if they're the arms of
the perfect person. And if, as you say, you do it with love in
your heart.

ZOEY.   Did I say that?

DON.
This is my perfect person right here. My life, my light, my
darling.
ELVIRA.

    This is rather startling.

    Is this a joke?

DON.

    No.

ELVIRA.

    More of the usual mirrors and smoke?

DON.

    An eleventh-hour confession.

ELVIRA.

    An admission. To wit?

DON.

    I love you, Elvira.

ELVIRA.

    Oh *shit!*

DON.

    If you have any doubt,

    Here and now I'll allay it.

    I love you, Elvira.

ELVIRA.

    It took you long enough to say it!

ZOEY.   Well, Mike. Now I know we're not in Illyria anymore.
(Don, Leporello and Sandy turn in surprise.)
SANDY.   Did you say ...
DON.   Illyria?
LEPORELLO.   Illyria?
SANDY.   Illyria?
ZOEY.   Illinois, my home. Actually, my foster home.
SANDY.   Oh...!
DON.   Oh...!
ZOEY.   Did I say something?
SANDY.   So you're an orphan?
ZOEY.   Yes, but I do hope to meet my parents someday in
this lifetime.
SANDY.   And how old are you?

ZOEY.   Twenty-three.

SANDY.   Oh...!

DON.   Oh ...

SANDY.   And your name is — ?

ZOEY.   Zoey.

SANDY.   Zoey. Do you know who your parents were?

ZOEY.   All I know is, my mother's name was Wendy. Or Sandy.

SANDY.   Oh my God. Oh ...

DON.   Oh ...

SANDY.   Oh...!

ZOEY.   Did I say something else?

SANDY.   *I'm* Wendy!

LEPORELLO.   Sandy.

SANDY.   Sandy.

ZOEY.   You mean...?

SANDY.   My baby!

ZOEY.   Mamma...? *(They embrace.)*

MIKE.   Wow. What a small world.

LEPORELLO.   What a small stage. Move over, will ya?

DON.   Ladies and gentleman, time is short and there's much to do. The fact is, I have to go away tonight on a very long trip — with this lady. If you and your mother might catch up somewhere in private ...

ZOEY.   We could go to our place, Mike.

MIKE.   *Our* place?

ZOEY.   Mine. For the night. Am I right, Mike?

MIKE.   Well ...

LEPORELLO.   Mike, don't look a gift horse in the orifice. An ancient Egyptian saying.

MIKE.   Oh. You're right, Zo.

ZOEY.   Well goodbye, Mr. Johnson. Thank you for everything.

DON.   My pleasure. *(Kisses Zoey's hand, then shakes Mike's.)* Goodbye, my dear. Goodbye, Mike. No hard feelings, I hope.

MIKE.   About what?

DON.   Good luck. *(They start out.)*

101

LEPORELLO.   *(Aside to Don.)* Donny, this is your kid. Aren't
you going to tell her?
DON.
Only to leave her?
> Sandy, my profoundest apologies.
> Treasure her for me. And never reveal me.
> I'm sure you know why.
SANDY.
> I do. And I thank you.
> Little did I think that all my misery
> Would yield this prize. Goodbye.
(To Leporello.)
> Now about this quick one ...
LEPORELLO.   You didn't believe that, did you, honey? —
Donny, is she great? The eyes of a *basilisk.*
ZOEY.   Are you coming, Mom?
SANDY.   Lefty? Are *you* coming?
LEPORELLO.
> Yeah. Uh, listen, my beehive.
> Could you come back in a while?
> Say, twelve-oh-five?
SANDY.
> Twelve-oh-five.
LEPORELLO.
> *Adios,* my transcendental one.
SANDY.
> *Au revoir.* My sentimental one.
(Sandy goes out with Zoey and Mike.)
LEPORELLO.   So the Sandy's of time have finally run out.
DON.   I am sorry, Leporello.
LEPORELLO.   No, please. We had half a millennium. Had
to happen sometime, right?
DON.   Thank you for everything, down the ages.
LEPORELLO.   Probably futile to ask for a raise. — Master?
DON.   My friend?
LEPORELLO.   I'm so scared.
DON.   I am too, Leporello. I am too. *(They embrace.)*

LEPORELLO.   Guess I better change into something cool.
(Leporello exits. A storm begins to brew.)
DON JUAN.
>Do you hear that storm, Elvira?
>That thunder is a fanfare. The final claxon.
>It's the driver of the eternal taxi,
>Honking on his horn.
ELVIRA.
>But Don Juan — you do realize
>If we do this deed you'll be dead.
DON JUAN.
>*We* will. Together and complete.
>But we only have the briefest while.
ELVIRA.
>I well recall your speedy style.
DON JUAN.
>This time, as much as we can, let's linger.
>Finger to finger, soul to soul ...
ELVIRA.
>Body to body ...
DON JUAN.
>Head to head.
ELVIRA.
>There's only one place for it, my sweet.
DON JUAN.
>You mean — ?
ELVIRA.
>Bed.
DON JUAN.
>Bed.
DON JUAN and ELVIRA.
>Bed.
(There is a thunderclap as Mephistopheles appears.)
MEPHISTOPHELES.
>Not so fast, my pretties. *(Cough.)*
>Trick or treat.
DON JUAN.
>You can't take us yet. I have ten minutes to go.

MEPHISTOPHELES.

Ah. But listen.

(Raises a finger. A church clock chimes loudly.)

It seems your clocks *were* a little slow.

Midnight.

DON JUAN.

Oh, all right, all right. So you won.

ELVIRA.

You always knew you would.

DON JUAN.

Checkmate.

MEPHISTOPHELES.

But what the heck, mate.

You were really *good*.

DON JUAN.

Good? Are you kidding?

MEPHISTOPHELES.

In roles that were terribly forbidding.

Elvira — superior.

Don Juan — I applaud your long run.

Sensational.

ELVIRA.

I'm glad we didn't defraud you of your fun.

MEPHISTOPHELES.

Fun? My dear, this was wildly educational.

Your determination in spite of distress.

This gentleman's politesse.

All those women requesting Fritos, seltzer, and ice

And he was always *unfailingly* nice.

A-plus.

A pity after all that work to reward you thus.

DON JUAN.

At least it's over now.

MEPHISTOPHELES.

I'm still hungry. I want more.

ELVIRA.

The more to torture us?

MEPHISTOPHELES.

No, no ...

DON JUAN.

You've waited centuries for this.

Why rejoice we lived so long?

MEPHISTOPHELES.

Why, for the same reason I signed you on.

DON JUAN.

Which wasn't generosity.

MEPHISTOPHELES.

Actually it was the basest curiosity.

I wanted to find out what *you'd* find out, Don Juan.

A man who'd sell his soul not to sweeten his tooth

But to dig in the mine of eternal truth,

To search for the very meaning of life!

I've lived a billion years and *I* can't unwind it.

I thought that, given time, *you* might find it.

DON JUAN.

All that time amid all that screwing

I never did one single thing worth doing.

You hoped in vain, Satan.

MEPHISTOPHELES.

Maybe the meaning of life isn't all that blatant,

For heaven's sake.

As for the meaning of death,

Well that's *really* opaque.

(Elvira kneels.)

ELVIRA.

Sir.

MEPHISTOPHELES.

Oh, please. Kneeling for mercy, madam?

Some pathetic petition?

ELVIRA.

The opposite, sir. I beg for perdition.

Though I should wander forever without home

I prefer eternal torment with this man

To immortality alone.

DON JUAN.   *(Kneels alongside Elvira.)*
> You would have had her anyway
> If the clocks had not been slow.

MEPHISTOPHELES.
> But tell me, sir:
> Why would you have lain with her
> Only to perish?

DON JUAN.
> Because I cherish her, of course.

MEPHISTOPHELES.
> Really, Don Juan,
> How can I cast you into eternal fire and ice?
> You'd spoil the place by being so terribly *nice*.
> A gentleman in hell? Very dicey, no mistake.
> And then what you did today — ?
> The icing on the cake.

DON JUAN.
> Today I reached absolute zero.

MEPHISTOPHELES.
> Sir, you sacrificed yourself for loved one and kin.
> Is that not the very definition of "hero"?

DON JUAN.
> I committed the gravest of sins.
> I threw my life away, a gift from the Invincible.

MEPHISTOPHELES.
> Yes, but you're throwing it away on *principle*.
> Which hardly savors of hellish behavior.
> And love —
> Love, which has always been a mystery to me
> I understand through you somehow ... viscerally.
> As God is in heaven above you,
> You might almost say you made me love you.
> Don Juan, for four centuries I have learned
> By looking through your eyes.
> And for this, tonight you'll be in paradise.

(He produces the contract and tears it up.)
> Behold. I free you.

DON JUAN.

Free me? But not me alone ...

MEPHISTOPHELES.

No, my reluctant Casanova.

Peerless Elvira, too.

DON JUAN.

And Leporello? For him too I plead.

MEPHISTOPHELES.

Leporello, I decree, shall live out his natural life

With Sandy his unnaturally well-analyzed wife.

(Leporello, Sandy, Zoey, and Mike appear.)

As for Zoey, your incandescent daughter,

A diamond of the first water,

This more than earthly prize

Will bring you glittering descendants

Granting you the immortality you sought

In a different guise.

Todd, whose name means death,

Shall walk the earth loveless and alone

Until his final heartless breath.

Arise, my friends.

Your time is over and ended your ancient quest.

DON JUAN.

What about eternal torment?

ELVIRA.

The fiery pit?

MEPHISTOPHELES.

A little test.

DON JUAN.

A *test?*

ELVIRA.

That's very breezy.

MEPHISTOPHELES.

This is *salvation.* Do you think it's *easy?*

No, not for you two the infernal abyss.

Prepare instead to meet eternal bliss.

Open, you heavens, your azure tent!

107

That these two may boff into infinity
To their heart's content!
(A mystical angelic chorus has begun to be heard.)
I shall miss you both terribly.
ELVIRA.
Is it possible?
DON JUAN.
We're not going to hell, then ...
MEPHISTOPHELES.
Heaven, my prince. Heaven!
The celestial palace!
Prepare to Don the aurora borealis!
I give you what I gave up in my horrific prison:
The knowledge of God, the beatific vision
With front-row seats!
While you're at it, give my best to Johnny Keats.
Angels are standing in ranks right now,
Archangels are trumpeting at the gate!
And I say unto you, my friends —
It was well worth the wait.
(The sky opens up to blinding light, and the heavenly chorus gets louder.)
Accipe, Domine, hos beatos homines in vitam aeternam, tecum vivant in caelo cum tuis angelis per saecula saeculorum!
Sanctus, sanctus, sanctus! Dominus Deus Sabaoth!
(His voice is drowned out by a deafening choir of angels, as Don and Elvira join hands and are taken into heaven. White wings sprout from Mephistopheles.)

THE END

TRANSLATIONS

DON JUAN

Sanguis melanchrys bovis atque caput avis ...
    Golden-black blood of an ox and head of a bird ...

Lingua serpentis et folium floris. Commiscite!
    Tongue of serpent and leaf of flower. Mix together!

Crepusculi pulvis et lacrima virginis ...
    Dust of twilight and tear of a virgin ...

Canis capillus et capillus regis. Admiscete!
    Hair of dog and hair of a king. Join together!

Ranae membrana et oculus felis. Incipite!
    Skin of frog and eye of cat. Begin!

Arcesso te! Advoco te! Impero te! Adesto!
    I summon you! I call on you! I order you! Be here!

In nomine omnium nefariorum imperiorum impero te! Coniuro te!
Appareat et surgat — Mephistophilis!
    In the name of all the impious empires I order you!
    I conjure you! Appear, rise up — Mephistopheles!

MEPHISTOPHELES

Redeo, ferae nefandae! Aperite, O portae! Recipe, O Tantare, tuum
regem! Accipe me — Mephistophelem!
    I return, abominable creatures! Open, O gates! Receive
    your king, O Hades! Take me! Mephistopheles!
Accipe, Domine, hos beatos homines in vitam aeternam, tecum
vivant in caelo cum tuis angelis per saecula saeculorum! Sanctus,
sanctus, sanctus! Dominus Deus Sabaoth!

109

Accept, Lord, these blessed beings into eternal life, may they live with you in heaven among your angels unto ages and ages! Holy, holy, holy! Lord God of Hosts!

PROPERTY LIST

Alchemical flasks with bubbling fluids
Food tray with toast (LEPORELLO)
Large hourglass
Alchemical book (DON JUAN)
Skull
Contract for Don Juan (MEPHISTOPHELES)
Contract for Dona Elvira (MEPHISTOPHELES)
Knife
Quill pen (MEPHISTOPHELES)
Fake dagger with retractable blade (DON JUAN)
Fake carving knife with retractable blade (DON JUAN)
Spanish fan (ELVIRA)
Silver creamer (DON JUAN)
Astrolabe
Handkerchief (MEPHISTOPHELES)
Sunglasses (DON JUAN, ELVIRA)
Cigarettes (SANDY)
Pair of lace panties (SANDY)
Wine bottle (LEPORELLO)
Bourbon bottle (LEPORELLO)
Wine and bourbon glasses (LEPORELLO)
Roll of condoms (DON JUAN)
Doctor's certificate (DON JUAN)
Blood test (DON JUAN)
Black book (LEPORELLO)
Umbrellas (TODD, DON JUAN)
Eyeglasses (TODD)
Tie (TODD)
Bag of Doritos chips
Volume of Keats poetry
Piece of candy (ZOEY)
Gift-wrapped tie box with paper tag (ZOEY)
Pesticide tank with hose (MEPHISTOPHELES)
Pistol (with blanks) (TODD)

COSTUME PLOT

ACT ONE

DON JUAN
Black doublet
Black pumpkin hose
Black tights with cod piece
Black suede slippers
Watch

LEPORELLO
Full Julliard shirt
Vest
Wool knee britches
Brown tights
Belt
Watch
Espadrilles

MEPHISTOPHELES
2-piece red Doublet and hose
Red velvet hat with feathers
Red tights
Red cape
Red shoes
Red tail
Horns
Belt with dagger

DONA ELVIRA
Cream dress with train and Julliard frontispieces, circa 1599
Julliard shawl
Creme knee-high stockings
Earrings

Necklace
Black curly wig
Silver shoes
Cream velvet bag
Cream fan on wrist ribbon

ACT TWO

DON JUAN
2-piece, 3-button black suit
White shirt
Clock tie
Black shoes
Sunglasses
Black belt with condoms

LEPORELLO
Gold T-shirt
Shorts
Belt
Espadrilles
Jacket

SANDY
2-piece teal suit
Cream blouse
Beige shoes
Stockings
Earrings
Raincoat

MIKE
Grey corduroy trousers
Blue plaid shirt
Sneakers
Denim jacket

ZOEY
Jeans
Sneakers
Beige shirt

TODD
Raincoat
Blue shirt
Tie
Shoes
Socks
Belt
Glasses

VERONICA BLISS
Louise Brooks wig
Black dress
Black jacket
Black stockings
Black patent-leather shoes
Earrings
Sunglasses

MEPHISTOPHELES
T-shirt with "Acme Pest Control"
Bra with pads
Black belt
Black mini skirt
Black wig
Fishnet stockings
Black high-heeled shoes

DON JUAN
2-piece, 3-button black suit
White shirt
Black shoes
Black belt with condoms
Overcoat

LEPORELLO
Gold T-shirt
Long pants
Belt
Espadrilles
Jacket

MIKE
Gray corduroy trousers
Blue-plaid shirt
Sneakers
Denim jacket

ZOEY
Flower dress
Sandals

MEPHISTOPHELES
2-piece red Doublet and hose
Red velvet hat with feathers
Red tights
Red cape
Red shoes
Red tail
Horns
Belt with dagger
White rose
Wings

SOUND EFFECTS

Thunder
Ominous rumbling of an approaching storm
Mystical chorus of voices
Deafening thunderclap
Doorbell
Clock chiming the hours
Phone ringing
Angelic chorus
Demonic chorus

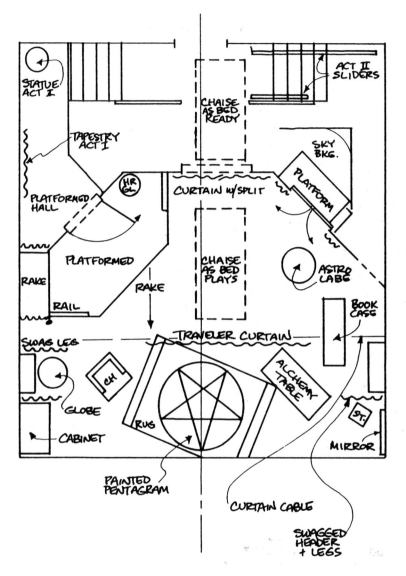

SCENE DESIGN

ACT ONE

"DON JUAN IN CHICAGO"

(DESIGNED BY BOB PHILLIPS FOR PRIMARY STAGES)

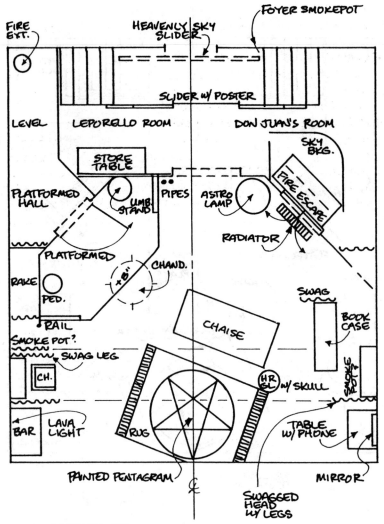

FOYER SMOKEPOT

FIRE EXT.

HEAVENLY SKY SLIDER

SLIDER w/ POSTER

LEVEL   LEPORELLO ROOM   DON JUAN'S ROOM

SKY BKG.

STORE TABLE

FIRE ESCAPE

PLATFORMED HALL   UMB. STAND   PIPES   ASTRO LAMP

RADIATOR

PLATFORMED

CHAND.

RAKE   "+8"   SWAG

PED.   BOOK CASE

RAIL

SMOKE POT?   CHAISE

SWAG LEG

CH.   HR GL w/ SKULL   SMOKE POTS

BAR   LAVA LIGHT   RUG   TABLE w/ PHONE

PAINTED PENTAGRAM   MIRROR

SWAGGED HEAD w/ LEGS

PROPERTY OF
HIGH POINT PUBLIC LIBRARY
HIGH POINT, NORTH CAROLINA

SCENE DESIGN
ACT TWO
"DON JUAN IN CHICAGO"
(DESIGNED BY BOB PHILLIPS FOR PRIMARY STAGES)